The Conversation Strategies Manual

A complete course to develop conversation skills

Alison Roberts

First published in 2012 by
Speechmark Publishing Ltd, Sunningdale House, Caldecotte Lake Business Park,
Milton Keynes MK7 8LF, UK
Tel: +44 (0)1908 277177 Fax: +44 (0)1908 278297
www.speechmark.net

© Alison Roberts, 2012

All rights reserved. The whole of this work, including all text and illustrations, is protected by copyright. No part of it may be copied, altered, adapted or otherwise exploited in any way without express prior permission, unless in accordance with the provisions of the Copyright Designs and Patents Act 1988 or in order to photocopy or make duplicating masters of those pages so indicated, without alteration and including copyright notices, for the express purpose of instruction and examination. No parts of this work may otherwise be loaded, stored, manipulated, reproduced, or transmitted in any form or by any means, electronic or mechanical, including photocopying and recording, or by any information storage and retrieval system, without prior written permission from the publisher, on behalf of the copyright owner.

002-5805/Printed in the United Kingdom by CMP (UK) Ltd

British Library Cataloguing in Publication Data

A catalogue record for this book is available from the British Library

ACKNOWLEDGEMENTS

Most authors will recognise that there is a degree of self-absorption in the act of writing a book, which tends to exclude other tasks! Thank you to my patient and helpful husband, Peter, and our children Amy, Faith and Tom (who co-wrote the chapter about electronic conversations).

Thanks also go to my Speech and Language Therapy colleagues at Good Communication, our small Speech and Language Therapy company, who have tried out some of the ideas in this book: Siobhan O'Brien, Marie Couch, Gemma Telling, Julia Stallabrass and Jinnie Goodlake.

CONTENTS

1. Introduction 1
2. Procedure 3
3. Greetings 7
4. Opening gambits 15
5. Introducing yourself 21
6. Remembering names 25
7. Mechanical rules 29
8. Formulaic interchanges 37
9. Formal and casual conversations 41
10. Body language 45
11. What are other people's interests? 53
12. Open and closed questions and invitations to speak 57
13. The www. technique 63
14. Choosing and introducing a conversation topic 67
15. Noticing, commenting and making polite observations 73
16. The Social CV 79
17. Using humour 93
18. Compliments 97
19. Criticism and complaints 103
20. Reminiscing and reflecting 109
21. Being optimistic 113
22. Being positive about other people 119
23. Argument, making a point and detachment from your opinions 123
24. Apologies and repairing conversational 'gaffes' 131
25. Escaping! 137
26. Electronic conversations 143
27. Eavesdropping 149
28. Conversation at parties and special occasions 153
29. The conversation 'menu' 161
30. Sayings and points to consider about conversations 165

Appendices

Appendix 1: The Conversation Strategies Checklist: self-assessment and log 167
Appendix 2: Question dice 181
Appendix 3: Save your cracker jokes 183
Bibliography and recommended further reading 185

INTRODUCTION

Social settings that require us to talk can feel unnerving to anyone. How will we greet people? What will we talk about? Will we be able to understand what they are talking about? In short, are we up to the task? Have we 'mastered the art of conversation' sufficiently to allow it to flow in a natural way?

Such doubts feed into almost everyone's shyness at some time in their lives, but there are people who fear social settings so much that they will avoid socialising wherever possible. At the same time they can feel lonely or in need of a friend. For some people their preference for being alone far outweighs their desire to be sociable, but practice in the skills needed to talk can help to make conversations easier. There are, after all, some situations where conversation is expected and keeping quiet is not an option.

This book sets out ideas for analysing and recording conversational abilities in a transparent way, alongside the client; suggests strategies and exercises to help improve confidence in conversations; offers photocopiable homework reminders the size of credit cards for each aspect of conversation being addressed, and provides a photocopiable template for a progress journal to be filled in by both the client and the therapist.

Some activities suggested in the book aim to help with getting conversations started, others include looking at the value of conversational questions and the skills of keeping a conversation going or drawing it to a close. One chapter aims to be a morale and confidence booster, another looks at the conversational codes used in different social settings and one looks at the general structure of conversations.

The book is written with Speech and Language Therapists in mind, to use as an assessment and therapy tool with clients who struggle to use, or understand, conversation techniques. However, each chapter is addressed to the client so that they may use the book themselves and so that therapy can become a collaborative venture. For many clients the best way of working with this book will be to discuss each chapter with the therapist, work with the activities suggested, complete the homework for each chapter, fill in the journal and then revise with the therapist. Please read the next section, 'Procedure', for more details.

PROCEDURE

Before you start

Please be aware of a key document in the Appendices: the Conversation Strategies Checklist (CSC), which is used both as a self-assessment tool and as a log for the client's experiences and reflections. It is there to help maximise the effectiveness of therapy and self-help.

The log part of the form asks the client to observe others using the strategy in question, date the observation, include a comment and then make a note of the date when they used the strategy, adding another comment where possible. This log forms a rolling self-assessment that makes progress clear. It is kept by the client and reviewed by the therapist from time to time. It is designed to be used in addition to the homework 'credit cards', but it is, of course, for the therapist and client to decide jointly how therapy is to proceed; these are just tools to help you.

The aim will be to reassess towards the end of the period of therapy.

Identifying the problem areas

Many clients feel uneasy about holding conversations, but are not sure where in the process things go wrong or how they could improve their skills and confidence. It is helpful to gather information from the client, as well as further details perhaps from a family member, partner or friend, and add information from observation of the client within the clinical setting and, where possible, in other social situations.

Begin by working with the individual client. Have ready a photocopy of the CSC and together consider and fill in the self-assessment scale for each item. If the client is unsure, look at the relevant chapter for more detail and further discuss whether that is something they need to tackle.

Often the client's own perspective gives sufficient information to pinpoint problem areas but sometimes they ask for the thoughts of others to be involved. Some clients prefer to fill in all or part of the CSC at home. The client and therapist should both keep a dated copy of the initial CSC results as a record of the baseline.

As work progresses the client may decide that they would, in fact, benefit from tackling some other aspects of conversation too. This information can be factored in later.

Where to start therapy

The CSC results may indicate that there are only a few areas requiring a lot of work, with other aspects of conversation just needing a little confidence-building. However, many clients like to work through all of the chapters from start to finish, and the first few chapters are often of interest to all clients; it has been found that working on them tends to raise confidence, and this helps the therapist to deepen their knowledge of the client's strengths and difficulties.

The order of the first chapters follows approximately the way a conversation proceeds – they are not necessarily progressive in levels of difficulty. Later chapters tackle specific areas of skill, and therapists and clients may want to pass a few sections by, to reach a particular aspect of conversation that is found to be difficult.

Please don't feel constrained by the written order; it's often a good idea just to 'dip in' here and there or to use the chapters in the way that meets the needs of your client.

Group therapy versus one-to-one

It is a good idea to encourage the client to participate in some group therapy sessions after the initial interview so that they can practise conversation in a more realistic setting, and may benefit fully from the suggested group therapy activities and games.

It would be a counsel of perfection to advise matching ages and types of client, but this is sometimes possible in a college setting. It is often found that working on aspects of conversation that were not on one client's list but on that of another group member can still be a helpful exercise for all, for the following reasons: as affirmation of their own ability; to benefit from the feeling of being able to help another client; or to discover that they could in fact do with a little more practice in an area they thought they had fully understood.

Therapists and clients may feel that after a few group therapy sessions some individual appointments are needed again to review, reassess and agree upon the next steps.

It is not always possible to form a group, but therapy can still be very effective in the one-to-one setting. Motivation is often particularly high in older clients who attend on an individual basis but with some sessions enhanced by the occasional presence of a partner, family member or friend. Individual clients will need to make even more use of the CSC log to show how they are tackling the skills outside the sessions. As therapy progresses they will also make use of the homework cards and feed back on those.

PROCEDURE

Session activities and homework

Therapeutic activities aim to balance interactive and reflective work, so that therapy does not become boring. They are mostly designed for small groups, but many are for one client plus the therapist. In addition to the discussions, role play scenarios and other activities suggested in each chapter, there are the homework 'credit cards', designed to help generalise into daily life the work started in the clinical sessions. Clients should be encouraged to report back information on their homework experiences.

Final chapters

The last two chapters are general discussion points and can be used at any point in the therapy course, as a break from more intense work or as the last session before a holiday.

GREETINGS

Self-assessment questionnaire

On a scale of 1–10, where 1 is difficult and 10 is easy, how do you feel about greeting:

- *just one friend of the same sex as you?*
- *just one friend of the opposite sex?*
- *a group of friends of the same sex as you?*
- *a group of friends of the opposite sex or a mix of males and females?*
- *new people in a familiar place, for example, at college/work?*
- *new people not 'on your territory' – perhaps in a pub or a waiting room?*

"Hi!", "Good morning!", "Hello!", "Good afternoon!"

Greeting a friend or family member whom you see every day can be comparatively easy – you may only need to give a small acknowledgement of their presence. But how will you greet several friends, work colleagues or fellow students at a break, or later at the pub? How do you tackle the greeting at the start of an interview? How do you manage the greetings that usually take place on the phone? What is the most appropriate way to greet a new girlfriend or boyfriend at an evening meal? Or his/her parents? How do you greet people at a sombre occasion or at a particularly happy one? How formal should you be or how casual?

A man I have met, who has Asperger's Syndrome, and is an excellent speaker on the subject of living with the condition, mentioned at one of his talks that he has a particular difficulty in approaching doors. He worries that there will be someone else approaching the door from the other side at the same time. The following questions are among those that bother him about this situation:

- *Should he make eye contact with the person?*
- *Should he greet them and if so what would be the appropriate greeting?*
- *How long should he talk with the person?*
- *Should he hold the door open for them if it's a woman? If it's a man?*

His concerns reflect the worries experienced by many shy people and by those on the autism spectrum when they meet people, not just in the 'door situation', but generally, for example, just how *do* you arrange your face and say the words of greeting?

In this chapter we look at styles of greeting, planning your approach and some practical therapy activities.

Styles of greeting

Any greeting is primarily an acknowledgment of the other person and how we feel about their presence at that moment. It is usually considered to be rude not to make any acknowledgement of another person.

Greetings graded in order of warmth are discussed below, from the barest minimum where we merely recognise that the other person, a stranger, is there, to the level where we are so overjoyed to see a friend/loved one that we will give them a hug or even a kiss. Consider the following grades of greeting:

1 A complete stranger
Make brief eye contact with the other person or people, putting on a pleasant face, although not quite smiling. This means that you are showing that you know they are there, but are not intending to become involved in a conversation. (For more information on eye contact please see the chapter 'Body language'.)

2 Someone you see from time to time, but haven't ever spoken to
Make eye contact and smile. This is a 'warm but brisk' greeting.

3 An acquaintance or someone you know slightly
Make brief eye contact, smile and say "Good morning" or just "Morning", "Hello", "Hi" and so on, and walk on swiftly. This indicates that you are quite pleased to see them, although you haven't time to chat at the moment.

4 Someone you know a bit better
Make fuller eye contact, smile, say "Good morning" and add their name, assuming you know it. (You may still decide to walk on, however.) This is much more specific and indicates that you are interested enough/have taken the trouble to remember their name. (For more information on remembering people's names please see the chapter 'Remembering names'.)

5 A neighbour or someone you are quite familiar with
Make eye contact, smile, greet, add their name and ask how they are. This does not invite them to give you a detailed explanation of their current health or relationship problems, and similarly if they ask you how you are they will not need details either.

GREETINGS

"How are you?" is simply a convention to indicate a polite interest in them. The usual reply is: "I'm fine, thanks, and you?" or "I'm good thanks, and you?"

6 A fairly close work colleague at work

Make eye contact, smile, say "Hi" or "Hello" informally, add their name and ask how they are, plus an appropriate supplementary question, such as: "Did you have a good weekend?" or, if you know they have been on holiday, say: "Did you have a good holiday?" You should expect that they would reciprocate by asking you about your weekend or holiday. For more detail on supplementary questions just after a greeting please see the next chapter, 'Opening gambits'.

So far the types of greeting have been in more or less cumulative stages. Now let's look at other aspects of greeting:

7 The formal setting, for example, an interview

In these settings we should expect to be making eye contact, greeting at level 4, and shaking hands. The handshake should have definite warmth, but not be crushingly firm.

8 The waiting room setting

If there are several people waiting then use the standard approach of making eye contact and smiling. The special technique needed here is in placing and spacing yourself appropriately in the room, with respect to the placement of other people also waiting. The trick is to sit so that people are distributed with equal spacing but not directly opposite each other. No one will actually get up and move to achieve this when someone enters or leaves the room, but it is a good idea to attempt to achieve equal spacing when you first enter. If there's just one other person in the room make eye contact, smile and say a quiet "Good morning/afternoon", and take care not to sit right next to them. (It's usually a good idea to pick up a magazine if there is one there and read that.) For more information on placing yourself in a room please see the chapter on 'Body language'.

9 The informal group – at a pub, party or similar setting

If you really dread walking into a room full of people then be early and be prepared to greet newcomers as they enter the room. However, if you are not the first then try the following:

In an unhurried way, smile warmly, taking in everyone, especially those who are making eye contact with you. Then say "Hello" or "Hi" to one or two people nearby, and give a particularly warm greeting to the person who is hosting this get-together. If you see anyone standing alone then this would be a good person to greet.

10 The really good friend who you have not seen for a long time

This could be an occasion for a hug and a really warm greeting such as: "How lovely to see you." (Don't forget the smile and eye contact first.)

11 A member of your family

This will depend on the warmth of your relationship with that person and the length of time since you last saw them. After just a day at work, a short, spoken greeting is good. After a week or so away from your Mum she probably deserves a hug and a kiss on the cheek, while Dad would most likely prefer a hug with a pat on the back. For brothers and sisters it depends on your family convention, but a basic rule would be that the longer you have been apart the warmer the greeting would be.

12 Your girlfriend/boyfriend

A gradually spreading smile, eye contact and spoken greeting should take place as you walk towards him/her. The variable points here are how deep the relationship is and where you are meeting. If you've already been out together without other people you would probably just say "Hello", adding an appropriate non-verbal greeting. Assuming you are meeting in a public place this would be a hug and a brief kiss on the cheek. Mouth-to-mouth kisses are better left for private times, as this is much less awkward for other people around.

A few extra notes

Reciprocate the other person's style of greeting. It would be seen as rude only to give a slight smile when your friend or relative is trying to give an enthusiastic hug. However, you should never feel you have to be touched in a way you dislike. Similarly, if they are giving a reserved smile to you, they may feel overwhelmed if you offer a hearty handshake or hug.

Handshakes

Watch on TV or observe in real life some handshakes with extras, such as: wrist-and-hand shaking; 'thumbs up' handshakes that are held at chest level; handshakes with the added warmth of a hand on the upper arm; 'High 5'; shoulder slapping; and Jamaican Handshakes (look this one up on YouTube). Only use these forms if you are confident that they are appropriate.

Cheek-to-cheek kissing

The rules for this are varied and can be confusing. The actual 'kiss' does not make contact with the other person's cheek, but is more of a kiss into the air, with an accompanying 'moi' sound by their ear. In some cultures the usual form is one kiss usually on the left cheek, but sometimes the right. Sometimes both cheeks are kissed and sometimes this is repeated. Your best bet is to wait for the other person to take the lead and fall in with what they are offering. However, if you dislike that kind of thing then the best way to deflect it is to stand further away and offer a handshake instead.

Greeting children

This can be difficult, and depends on the age of the child and how well you already know them. If you don't know a child, and they are on their own, then it's best not to greet them at all. However, if you do know them or they are accompanied by someone you know, the best plan is just to smile, make eye contact and say hello, adding their name if you know it. If the child is very young, seems shy or you are not acquainted then greet the accompanying adult, and just include the child in your smile and eye contact. If you feel confident that the accompanying adult expects it, then greet their child more warmly by squatting or bending down so that you are at their level (but at arm's length away), and giving the usual smile, eye contact and greeting.

Try these exercises

- **Scenarios**

    In your group discuss and briefly role play or practise the scenarios 1–12 mentioned earlier. OK, maybe not the girlfriend/boyfriend one!

- **Non-Verbal Greeting Circle**

    A social language group can try the 'Non-verbal greeting circle'. This means that you say hello to each other around the circle, using only non-verbal methods, for example, handshake, wave, pat on the shoulder, 'High 5', thumbs up or broad grin. (This exercise is also useful as a part of the work on body language.)

- **Verbal Greeting Circle**

    Now try the 'Verbal greeting circle', that is, greeting in as many verbal ways as you can think of, for example, "Hi", "Hello" or "Good morning". Also try to make a note of the kind of person you could greet in that way, for example, you could use "Hi" with a friend, but probably not with a bank manager or head teacher.

- **Greetings Game**

    Make three sets of written cards using different colours for each set:

    Set 1, red set – Types of people including: various relatives (eg sister, granny, long-lost uncle), friends (eg individual, groups, school friends, girlfriend/boyfriend, work colleagues), authority figures (eg boss, doctor, head teacher) unexpected, unlikely or fantasy persons (eg film stars, MPs, sports celebrities, aliens).

Set 2, green set – Situations where the meeting takes place, for example, at a party, at a relative's wedding, in a museum, in the street, on a bus or train, at the dentist's.

Set 3, yellow set – 'Wild cards' – which will make each meeting different, such as: 'This is the first time you have met this person since they returned from a long holiday.'; 'You met this person a few moments ago and now meet them again.'; 'There is loud music.'; 'You meet this person unexpectedly.'; 'You have been avoiding this person but now it would be awkward not to chat to them.'; 'This is your first meeting, you do not like the look of this person.'

The activity is to take it in turns firstly to pick up a Set 1 red card and tell the group who you are speaking to. Then pick up one of each of the other types of card, tell the group what the card says, and greet the person in the appropriate way, bearing in mind the situation and unusual circumstances. You will need to think about the situation, and decide which 'code' or 'register' is appropriate. This means whether to adopt a 'matey', friendly but thoughtful, or formal style. Discuss your performance with the other group members.

Variation – every member of the group picks up a red card at the same time and pretends to be that character, displaying the card on the table or pinned to their chest. Now one group member picks a green card to form a social scenario in which all the characters greet each other in the appropriate way. This is hard work but good fun.

GREETINGS

Greetings 'credit cards' for homework

> Today I'm going to watch a TV interview and a TV drama programme or 'soap'. I'll look out for styles of greeting and report my findings at the next therapy session.

> Today I'm going to try greeting members of my family/my household who I meet either at breakfast or when I come home after work.

> Today I'm going to try greeting someone I know slightly. I'll make full eye contact, smile, say "Good morning" and add their name.

> Today I'm going to try greeting my neighbour or a fairly close work colleague. I'll make eye contact, smile, say "Hi" or "Hello", add their name and ask how they are, and add something else, such as asking if they had a good weekend/holiday.

> Today I'm going to meet a really good friend who I haven't seen for a long time. I'll try a hug, if they seem to welcome it, and a really warm greeting such as: "How lovely to see you."

> Today I'll try greeting a group of friends at a pub. I'll walk into the room in an unhurried way, I'll let my smile broaden and grow as I take in everyone. I'll say "Hello" or "Hi" to one or two people nearby and give a warm greeting to the host of this get-together, remembering to include their name. If I see anyone standing alone I'll try to greet them separately.

OPENING GAMBITS

Self-assessment questionnaire

On a scale of 1–10, where 1 is difficult and 10 is easy, how do you feel about making opening gambits with:

- *just one friend of the same sex as you?*
- *just one friend of the opposite sex?*
- *a group of friends of the same sex as you who have learning disabilities and need work on conversation, assertiveness and relationship skills?*
- *a group of friends of the opposite sex or a mix of males and females?*
- *new people in a familiar place, for example, at college/work?*
- *new people not 'on your territory' – perhaps in a pub or a waiting room?*

This chapter is an extension of the last and aims to overlap slightly. Congratulations if you now feel confident with greetings; this means you will already know how to begin to 'break the ice'. Now you are working towards getting the socialising going. At this point you may find it comforting, and a real confidence booster, to have a few flexible ideas ready for the initial exchanges.

Ideas for the extended conversation come later in the book, but for now, you need a few opening gambits. Try to avoid the temptation to have a very firm conversation plan that you feel the need to stick to at all costs, because your conversation partner may have ideas of their own which are different from yours.

Let's assume you have already greeted the person and now you need to follow up with another comment or question. This part of the chat forms a bridge between the greeting and the main part of the talking.

For opening gambits your most useful topic (in the UK anyway!) will be the weather and/or the seasons. There is almost always something to say about those. A tip – it's often a good idea to include or end your comment with a 'tag question', which is really to ask the conversation partner to agree with you: "There's a real touch of spring in the air, *isn't there*?"/"Looks like the start of winter, *doesn't it*?"/"I wonder whether it will rain, it's a bit cloudy today, *isn't it*?"

So the whole greeting and opening gambit might sound something like this: "Morning Bob. How are you?" Pause while he greets you and asks you how you are. Then you could add: "Lovely day today, isn't it?"

Wait for a response to your 'weather comment'. Then, if the other person doesn't expand on it or add their own conversational thread, you can, as mentioned in 'Greetings', ask about a recent event you know they have attended or participated in, for example, a half-term break, a conference, a party, a meeting or a wedding.

Try these exercises

- **Mind Maps or Visual Organisers**
  Fill in Mind Maps or Visual Organisers like the ones at the end of this chapter, to help with appropriate opening gambits, that is, things to say after the initial greeting words, for lots of different situations:

  - *coffee break at work*
  - *gardening club*
  - *nightclubs*
  - *a wedding*
  - *an interview for a job*
  - *a phone call with a new girlfriend/boyfriend*
  - *a funeral*
  - *a party with some friends you haven't seen for ages*
  - *your five-year-old niece.*

- **Verbal Greeting Circle**
  Try an extended 'Verbal greeting circle', that is, greeting and then adding an 'opening gambit' in as many verbal ways as you can think of, for example: "Hi, it's a great day, isn't it?", "Hello, how was the weekend in Birmingham?", "Good morning, how's your cold now?"

- **Extended Greetings Game**
  Use the Greetings Game cards described in the previous chapter, 'Greetings', with the three sets: Set 1 – Types of people; Set 2 – Situations where the meeting takes place, and Set 3 – 'Wild cards'.

Again take it in turns to pick up one of each type of card and greet that person in the appropriate way, bearing in mind the situation and any unusual circumstances, and adopting the appropriate 'code' or 'register'.

The difference, in this extended form of the game, is that you have to add an opening gambit.

Now another person in the group responds to the greeting and opening gambit with an appropriate response.

- **Opening Gambits with Children**
 You don't need too much of a run-up to a conversation with a child, just ask about a topic such as their school or recent holiday. Don't expect very lengthy answers from children, but to make them as long as possible by asking 'open questions', for example: "What was the best part of your holiday?" will get a longer reply than: 'Did you have a nice holiday?". See the chapter on 'Open and closed questions and invitations to speak' for more information.

Opening gambits 'credit cards' for homework

> Today I'm going to try a greeting plus an opening gambit with a member of my family, when I come home after work/college/shopping.

> Today I'm going to try a greeting plus an opening gambit at coffee or tea break at work.

> Today I'm going to try a greeting plus an opening gambit with my neighbour.

> Today I'm going to try a greeting plus an opening gambit at a social event (for example, a party, evening class or meeting with friends at a pub).

> Today I'm going to try a greeting plus an opening gambit at the start of a phone call with a new friend.

> Today I'm going to try a greeting plus an opening gambit when I've just met my friend who is going to the cinema with me. It needs to be a short comment as the film starts soon.

OPENING GAMBITS

Coffee break at work

- Bit cold this morning, isn't it?
- Had a good morning so far?
- How's your dad/child etc? Bit better?
- Did you have a good weekend?
- Did you see.... on TV last night?
- Nice and bright today isn't it?
- I noticed you've had a busy morning, you must be whacked?
- I wonder if that inspector is coming back. He looked a bit gloomy didn't he?

The Conversation Strategies Manual

Tea break at the gardening club

- How was the party?
- Are you going to that Open Garden next weekend?
- How did you get on with those free bulbs?
- Lovely weather for gardening, isn't it?
- How's your mum/child etc? Any better?
- Looks as if we're in for some rain, doesn't it?
- Are thay going to send us that magazine?
- Are you managing to get away this summer?

INTRODUCING YOURSELF

Self-assessment questionnaire

On a scale of 1–10, where 1 is difficult and 10 is easy, how do you feel about introducing yourself to:

- *a peer of either sex?*

- *other age groups (including children)?*

- *authority figures?*

In a social setting, such as a party, somebody, perhaps the host, will often introduce the guests to each other. However, if that does not happen, you may leave the party without the name of a person who you might have liked to contact in the future. (Think of Cinderella and all that business with the shoe, when a simple introduction might have solved the problem much more easily!) You will not be able to exchange names unless one of you starts the process, so why not let it be you? It is often a good idea to greet and give your name first, this way the person you are meeting will get the hint that they should respond by giving their name to you.

When we introduce ourselves it is possible to feel quite shy or to worry that we are not a match to our conversation partner. There are lots of good things about you (please see the chapter on 'The Social CV'), so there is no need to lack confidence. If you practise the following exercises on introducing yourself you will be able to *appear* confident even if this is really just an act. You need to say your name in such a way as to convey that you are content with who you are, but not arrogant.

Think of how you would like this person to address you now and in the future, so if you don't really like being called 'Elizabeth' but would prefer 'Liz' or 'Beth', or whatever, use that from the start. At a job interview you will need to include your surname, but you can still abbreviate your first name.

You might like to add a little more information along with your name, to help your listener to put you in context, for example: "Hi, my name's Samantha, I'm a student at college", or "Hi, I'm Philippa, I think we met at the conference last May", or "Hello, I'm Alex, I work with Bob in the IT department", or "I'm Kirsty, I know (name of party host) through our local History Society." More formally and on the phone you could try:

The Conversation Strategies Manual

"Hello, my name is Victor Meldrew, I phoned you yesterday, and the day before, about a problem with my drains."

Try these exercises

In a group setting try these exercises in pairs:

- **Name and Nickname**
  Just practise saying your name on its own. Try it in a soft voice, then loudly. Try just your first name, or nickname, and also your full name. Look in a mirror as you are saying the words and check that you are smiling. If you don't actually like your name, frequent repetition can help you to become more comfortable in saying it or you might decide to use your nickname instead.

- **Name +**
  Practise greeting and then adding the introduction: "Hello, my name is …"; "Good evening, I'm …"

- **About Yourself**
  Practise greeting, adding the introduction and adding some information about yourself.

- **I Know You**
  Practise greeting, adding the introduction and then clarifying how you know the host/hostess.

- **Victor Meldrew**
  Practise the 'Victor Meldrew' complaint type of scenario mentioned at the end of the paragraph above these exercises, taking care not to sound as pompous as the TV version (and, of course, use your own name!).

- **Putting it Together**
  Role play greeting then introducing yourself to the whole group in these ways:
  - *loudly, as if at a noisy party*
  - *softly but cheerily, as if in church at a wedding*
  - *in a straightforward, but gentle and quiet way, as if at a funeral*
  - *formally, as if at an interview.*

INTRODUCING YOURSELF

Introducing yourself 'credit cards' for homework

> Today I'm going to watch a 'soap' or other drama on TV, and look out for characters greeting and introducing themselves to one another.

> Today I'm going to try greeting and introducing myself to the friend of my relative.

> Today I'm going to try greeting and introducing myself to a neighbour or someone new at work.

> Today I'm going to try greeting and introducing myself to a person at a party.

> Today I'm going to try greeting and introducing myself to the friend of my friend.

> Today I'm going to try phoning to make a complaint. This will involve greeting and setting myself in context before coming to the main point of the phone call. If I haven't really got anything to complain about I'll wait until the next available opportunity. In the meantime I'll just practise this scenario.

REMEMBERING NAMES

6

Self-assessment questionnaire

On a scale of 1–10, where 1 is difficult and 10 is easy, how do you feel about:

- *remembering your conversation partner's name and using it during a social setting?*

- *remembering and using the speaker's name quite often during a phone conversation?*

- *remembering the name for the next time you meet?*

This chapter relates to the previous one about introducing yourself to someone else. Here we look at the situation of hearing and then remembering someone's name. These are skills worth cultivating because:

In a social situation when you use a person's name you show that you have been interested enough to focus your attention on them at the introduction. Dale Carnegie (*How to Win Friends and Influence People*) says: "Remember that a person's name is to that person the sweetest and most important sound in any language."

- If you know a person's name you will be able to introduce them to someone else.

- In a formal setting such as an interview you show respect by using the interviewer's name several times.

- If making a complaint you demonstrate that you have stored away that person's name for later use.

It is usual for people to introduce two people to each other in a form such as this: "Hilary, I'd like you to meet Tim. Tim this is Hilary." This is rather formal, but it's useful when others use it, because you have two chances of hearing and remembering the name. If you remember to introduce others in this way you will be helping the general friendliness of the social gathering. Often other useful details are added such as: "You both work in the IT department."

A few extra notes

If you did not hear someone's name properly or forget it immediately, it's best to say: "I'm sorry, I didn't quite catch your name", and then, as soon as you are confident you have the name correctly, repeat it quietly, and then use it again in the conversation as soon as you can. Another technique to use, when you forget a name but remember it as a bit complicated, is to ask the person to spell it for you and try hard to picture the name written down. Some people also recommend 'writing' the name in the air, but be aware that, if this is a technique that seems to help your memory, it's best to do it inconspicuously otherwise you run the risk of looking silly!

Try always to have a small notebook and pen handy so that (at a suitable moment *away from the social scene*) you can jot down names and something that reminds you of which name goes with which person (eg 'Jane Longford – nurse, long brown hair, wearing a blue dress, likes cats. Bernie Hayes – energy consultant, has to keep going outside for a smoke. Claire Webber, wears glasses, works in IT').

If there isn't a suitable moment to slip away and write names down, then try a visualisation strategy, backing it up later with the written note of the name and something to remind you. The visualisation, or 'picture it and think it', technique involves picturing the person in your mind, along with a mental image of their name in writing and anything that links the person to the name (eg Jane Longford – long hair, Bernie Hayes – sounds like burnt haze [smokes], Claire Webber – often looks clearly at websites [IT]).

You might try using rhyme as the association. This works especially well for first names, for example *Sue* rhymes with *shoe*, *Ben* rhymes with *10*, *Peter* rhymes with *heater*, *Nancy* with *fancy*, *Craig* with *vague*, *Mark* with *shark*, *Bruce* with *goose*. Beware of 'dangerous' rhymes such as *Mary* and *hairy*, in case you accidentally say the wrong one!

Try these exercises

- **Photos and Names**
  Collect 20 or more magazine or newspaper pictures of people in action. As a group invent for each depicted individual a name that links to the person either via their job or their appearance. It doesn't matter how silly the association is as long as it works. So, if there's a picture of a man fishing you could call him Sam Pike; an accountant might be Bill Price; a lady walking might be Heather Moor. A tall lady wearing a light-blue dress might be Claire Sky. One with steel-rimmed spectacles might be Stella Broadview. See for how long you can remember the names you have chosen. Try looking at the pictures again at the next session to test whether you can remember some of the names.

REMEMBERING NAMES

- **Jobs and Names**

  This exercise is best tried in a group of five or six people. Each person chooses an occupation and a made-up name. Role play a party introduction – introduce yourself and then wait with an expectant facial expression – usually the other person will oblige by supplying their name. If not, try "I'm … and you are …?" Try to find out their occupation too. Introduce yourself to three people, and then see if you can remember their character names and jobs. Talk to the other three and try to form any mental links between the faces and the invented names (not their jobs this time). Discuss who finds it easier to link the person's appearance with their name and who finds the job/name link easier to remember.

- **Star Names**

  Look at pictures of celebrities, living or dead, and decide on ways to remember their names. Again it can be as silly as you like; for example, Anthony Hopkins you might picture with ant bites on his toe and knee, and hopping about. You might picture Julia Roberts wearing lots of jewels that she has robbed (not in real life, but in a film setting, of course). Dustin Hoffman would be dusting the sculpture of a man. Ben Stiller would be bending to attend to glass tubes which are distilling alcohol.

Remembering names 'credit cards' for homework

> Today I'm going to try to learn and remember the names of two TV actors and the programmes in which I saw them. I'll think of appearance/name associations or job/name associations. I'll report my ideas back to the group.

> Today I'm going to try to learn and remember the names of two politicians (preferably cabinet ministers), the political parties they belong to and one thing they stand for. I'll think of appearance/name associations or job/name associations. I'll report my ideas back to the group.

> Today I'm going to try to learn and remember the names of two film stars and the films in which I saw them. I'll think of appearance/name associations or job/name associations. I'll report my ideas back to the group.

> Today I'm going to try to learn and remember the name of a new person at work/college. I plan to say the name straight after I've been told it and then use it in the conversation. I'll report my success back to the group.

> Today I'm going to phone an organisation to make an enquiry. I plan to learn the name of the person who I speak to and use the name in the conversation. I'll report my success back to the group.

> Today I'm going to phone an organisation to make a complaint. I plan to learn the name of the person who I speak to and use the name often in the conversation. I'll report my success back to the group.

MECHANICAL RULES

Self-assessment questionnaire

On a scale of 1–10, where 1 is difficult and 10 is easy, how do you feel about following basic 'mechanical rules' of conversations such as:

- *being in the right place for a conversation?*
- *understanding the conversation partner and asking for clarification?*
- *avoiding interruptions (in both directions, ie where they interrupt you and where you find yourself interrupting them)?*
- *taking turns of the right length?*
- *staying on the subject versus introducing a new topic?*
- *linking your comment to the preceding one?*

Conversation is not a mechanism, and talking with people cannot be reduced to a set of gears and pistons. However, even when people like their conversation partners, want to be polite, and have the will and imagination for the chat to go well, things can still go wrong. This is usually connected with problems over conversation rules or 'mechanics'. We need to be able to respond to conversation in a way that other people understand and expect, rather than leave them feeling puzzled and confused. This chapter looks at some fairly simple ways to improve the chances of a good conversation by understanding and practising the mechanical rules.

Conversation venues and locations

Sometimes conversations fail for very simple and basic reasons to do with the conditions in which the interaction takes place: the participants are trying to talk against background noise; one participant is short of time; the conversation partners are trying but failing to combine the chat with an activity such as work; or the conversation is attempted outside, where it could be too cold, or perhaps too warm, to stand and chat.

We often need to adjust our speaking style according to a particular venue, location or occasion. For example, you will need a louder voice and more active listening for talking and listening in a busy street, shopping arcade or market, but you will have to talk very quietly or even whisper if you need to chat in a church or library.

Understanding the conversation partner

Sometimes one conversation partner just misunderstands the other. This can lead to puzzlement or even argument. A very important point about conversation 'mechanics' is to do with making sure you are responding in the appropriate way. If you didn't hear your conversation partner's answer properly or didn't understand it, then ask them to repeat or clarify what they meant. Don't pretend to have understood if you haven't, this will only lead to a conversational muddle.

Sometimes people do not understand ambiguous language such as hints; these people are more straightforward. It's best to be clear when, for example, you find a room too cold. If you say: "Would you like me to put the heating on?" the straightforward person might say: "No thanks" (because they are warm) when really the need is to say: "Oh, yes of course, are you feeling a bit cold?"

Avoiding interruptions and when to 'chip in'

Sometimes conversation participants interrupt each other or take too long a conversational turn. These problems usually occur when the participants in the conversation are insufficiently aware of each other or not adequately listening.

A problem of awkwardness can arise for some people if speakers leave unexpectedly long empty gaps between comments. Some people find that encountering too many awkward conversational gaps can become a reason to fear or avoid subsequent conversations.

How do you know when it's a good moment to take your turn in a chat? Sometimes there is the really obvious cue – they ask you a question. However, often the other person will pause and/or make momentary eye contact with you, and this is a more subtle invitation for you to add a comment. One difficulty can be when the conversation partner just ploughs on with what they are saying, so that what started as an exchange of ideas becomes a monologue. In this case you will need to prepare your comment, look for a tiny gap, and ... go for it! You can signal your intention to speak by adding over their words a "mm, mm," sound, maybe also nodding your head.

It sometimes takes a while to 'tune in' to another person's conversational style, so take a few moments to work out where the natural breaks tend to occur in this person's chat.

There are some occasions when it is perfectly OK to interrupt someone's flow of conversation, if you can find a small opportunity to 'chip in' with a comment. Times when you can interrupt could be, for example, when something urgent has occurred: "The teacher you are talking about is just coming into the room"; or maybe when

MECHANICAL RULES

something incorrect is being said: "Actually, before you go any further, it couldn't have been her, she wasn't at that party, she was at a concert with me."

In a group conversation it is not only polite to allow others to take their turn in the chat, it's also important that you take up your own turn when it's offered or seems appropriate, otherwise your opinion will not be aired and people may wonder why you are not participating. Similarly, if you notice that a person in the group is not managing to get a word in edgeways you can help them by asking what they think about the topic.

In a chat with just one other person it's also important to take up your turn, otherwise there could be a long gap in the conversation, which can sometimes be a problem.

Try to think of a conversation as a game of ping-pong: each speaker keeping the ball on their side of the net for roughly the same length of time, batting it back to the other speaker, waiting for the bounce before returning it and, of course, using the same ball. Imagine what would happen if you were to ignore the ball coming towards you, bat it back before it bounced or bring in another ball at the same time! Note that the ball is batted to the other person, rather than at them, and compare the idea of talking to and talking at someone (discuss that in the group). Also, would it still be a game of ping-pong if neither participant actually served the ball?

Avoiding interruptions – How to avoid being interrupted

There are a few tricks on how to keep going when an interruption seems likely or when the conversation partner is a known interrupter! It's worth remembering that some other people are not good at turn-taking. If you have a problem talking to a particular person, it doesn't necessarily mean that you are the one with the poor understanding of conversational rules, it might be a problem with the other person, so don't be downhearted.

When you come to the end of a sentence but want to add to your previous comments, be careful not to finish with a gap, or to use an intonation pattern that descends or in any way appears to be 'petering out' and therefore inviting a comment from the other person. If you have not quite formulated what you want to say next try using a 'filler' such as "and also …" or "and I just wanted to add …" You could also just try continuing to talk assertively and with perhaps a slightly louder voice, but don't let yourself appear too dominant.

If you can plan your words ahead, you can use the trick employed by lots of politicians – they add at the start of their speech a proposed number of items, usually three, that they are going to talk about. Outside political circles you can still use this technique, it could be something like: "I think that's a great idea of yours, for three reasons; if we set off early we'll beat the traffic, we'll have time to get a coffee on the way and also it's nice to be early so we can get a seat in a good place."

Turn length

Perhaps success in a conversation is measured in terms of the participants coming away feeling happy. Their happiness partly depends on each speaker getting the right turn length, they feel they have had their fair share of the conversational cake. You should aim for a roughly equal length of time for each conversation partner, in the one-to-one setting or in a group. If you listen to a drama on TV you will probably find that the average conversational turn length is much shorter than you would expect (about 11 seconds). People don't want to hear long instructions in a typical conversation; neither do they want to have the complete history of your weekend activities or your detailed opinions about a film you saw. Short comments are a better bet; a conversation partner will ask you for more if they want to hear more. You can usually tell if a person is bored with what you are saying because they will look away, fidget a bit or check the time! (On the phone you'll have to listen for clues like pauses, the sounds of computers being turned on and so on, to become aware that your listener's interest has dwindled.)

A good general rule is to aim to spend more time hearing about the other person than about yourself. To make this easier a successful rule is: you ask two linked questions and listen to the responses, you then follow up with a comment to show you were listening and another to show you are on the same wavelength, for example: "Did you have a good weekend?" (wait for their reply); "What did you think of the beach there?" (they reply again); then show you are listening: "How lovely for you" and show you are on the same wavelength, for example: "Yes we went there once, and it was sunny when we went too."

Some conversationalists favour filling every gap in the conversation while others are fine with a 'comfortable silence'. Try to be sensitive to your conversation partner's needs regarding silences; if things go quiet try out one or two comments or questions but don't force chat.

The seamless link

Imagine yourself enthusiastically talking about a football game you saw on TV last night. Your conversation partner suddenly starts talking about their neighbour's curtains! How confusing would that feel? How hurtful? It would seem as if they were either not listening at all or were bored with you, or didn't understand what you were saying. In the same way, it's important not to switch topics too suddenly when you take up your own turn in a conversation or talk about things that are off the topic currently under discussion. The aim is to make a smooth transition from one conversational comment to the next, rather in the same way as radio magazine commentators will try to make a seamless link

MECHANICAL RULES

between one item and the next. The chapter on Choosing and introducing a conversation topic, has much more detail on this.

Topic shifting

Has it been a problem if you have something that you really want to talk about but are not quite sure when and how to introduce the topic into the conversation? This skill involves waiting for the right moment to introduce it. There are two approaches to this technique: you can link it to something already under discussion, by subtle topic shifting, or by direct introduction: "There's something I just wanted your opinion about …"

How long do conversations last?

Please see 'The conversation 'menu'' chapter for conversation frameworks that can be shrunk or stretched to fit the time available, but you should be able to get a rough plan to fit into even a short time.

Conversation time varies. A conversation at a coffee break could be the same length as the break itself, say 15 minutes, but more commonly might stop after perhaps five minutes, leaving time for people to read a part of their newspaper.

A conversation over a meal with one person will also tend to last as long as the meal, split up into separate mini chats on different topics and comments about the meal, with intervening pauses.

A conversation with old friends who you have invited for the evening may last for the evening, but may also be split into separate, shorter chats with individuals, some whole-group chats, and some that start, stop while people eat or drink, and then resume later.

On the phone it's best not to force the conversation to last more than about 5 – 10 minutes, because people might have other things to do. On the other hand, it's usually best to expand the conversation beyond just giving or receiving information, especially if it is someone you know fairly well.

Try these exercises

- **Timing the Chat**

    In your one-to-one session, or in your group, watch a recording of part of a TV programme where there are conversational interchanges. 'Soaps' are often best for this. Have a stopwatch handy and time the average turn length in say a 10-minute clip. Afterwards have a conversation on a topic set by the speech and language therapist and aim for everyone's turn length to be the same as the average you heard on the TV programme.

- **Just a Minute**
  Listen to a recording of 'Just a Minute' (BBC Radio 4 or on CD) together. Now try playing the game yourselves. The subject will be set by the therapist and one person talks about the subject without hesitation, deviation or repetition, until they are challenged by another player who then takes up the same topic for the remainder of the minute. You will need a stopwatch. If you would like to, although this is not really necessary, you can use scoring – one point for a correct challenge, one point for talking for a whole minute and others at the therapist's discretion! In a discussion afterwards consider whether a minute was too long. Try the game again, timing it for just half a minute or even a quarter of a minute.

- **Interruptions**
  Listen to a recording of a radio interview together – 'Today' on Radio 4 is a particularly good example – or a TV equivalent – for example, 'Newsnight' is also quite good for this purpose. These are often hard-hitting programmes where a very experienced interviewer is trying to gain a particular piece information from a politician, while the politician is trying to avoid this and convey a different point. Listen to the way the interviewer will interrupt repeatedly. Discuss whether the interview is successful in achieving the interviewer's goal or whether the number of interruptions meant that the style of interview was too irritating for the audience to listen to.

- **Three Points**
  Listen to a political interview together and try to notice any 'three-point answers', such as: "Our party has taken the right approach on this because – we know children are missing out; we know parents want the best for their children; we know that teachers have the answers." Try some conversational interchanges based on three-point answers.

- **2qr**
  Practise balancing the time spent on talking about yourself with that spent on talking about your conversation partner. A successful rule is: two questions plus a response ('2qr'), followed by another comment that relates back to you, to show you were listening and are on the same wavelength, for example: "Did you have a good weekend?" (wait for their reply); "What did you think of the beach there?" (they reply again); "How lovely for you."; and a short, linked comment about yourself, for example: "Yes we went there once, and it was sunny when we went too." Try this system in the group. You will need to role play conversations, taking turns so that

everyone has a chance to be the one asking the questions and also has the chance to be the responder in a set-piece conversation where the rules are applied as above – how does this feel? In real-life conversations the conversation partner will have their own agenda, but the outline plan is the same – make sure they have at least as much time talking to you as you have had talking to them.

- **Connections**
  Try a game of 'Connections'. This game really requires a small group although it could just be played by the therapist and the client. It requires no materials, but involves one person saying one word, and then the other saying something linked: "Sausages, KETCHUP, red, POST BOX, letters, STAMPS, foot, SHOE, boots, CHEMIST" and so on. You'll see that some connections change meaning, for example, the word 'stamps' changes from the thing you stick on an envelope to the act of stamping the foot. This is a background skill to staying on the subject and also shifting topics. It promotes the core idea of listening carefully.

- **Intonation**
  Practise saying a sentence such as: "I think it looks as if it's going to rain" in a way that (1) expects a response, delivered on a rising tone, and (2) expects no response, delivered on a falling tone. In the group discuss these intonation patterns and how strong the invitation is to respond, then try the same effect with lots of other sentences.

- **Yes, No and a Laugh**
  It is sometimes said that if you really can't or don't want to respond to someone talking at length in a conversation you can always try the 'Yes, no and a laugh' system. This means that the first time they pause you say "Yes", the next time "No" and at the third time you laugh briefly. Try this out in the group session and see where it works and where it could cause problems – it's definitely not recommended under normal circumstances!

Mechanical rules 'credit cards' for homework

Today I'm going to listen to a TV 'soap', think about the average conversational turn length taken by the characters and recall what was said in the SLT session about this.	Today I'm going to listen to a radio or TV interview, watch out for interruptions by the interviewer and think about how this might sound to the audience.
Today I'll listen to two other people talking. I'll note whether either interrupted and how the other person dealt with this. Did they allow themselves to be interrupted or did they 'talk over' the interrupter and keep going with their point?	Today I'm going to try to have a conversation with a group of colleagues or friends and try not to interrupt anyone.
Today I'm going to try to have a conversation with a group of colleagues or friends and try to find opportunities to chip in with a comment.	Today I'm going to try, on my own, to time myself talking about something in the news, for 10 seconds, then 30 seconds, then a minute.

FORMULAIC INTERCHANGES

Self-assessment questionnaire

On a scale of 1–10, where 1 is difficult and 10 is easy, how do you feel about the everyday, brief, semi-social exchanges of words with the following people:

- *a shop assistant?*
- *a person on the street who would like you to donate money for a good cause?*
- *a person next to you in a long queue?*
- *a fellow passenger on a train that has stopped for no apparent reason?*
- *a waiter?*
- *a taxi-driver?*
- *your hairdresser/barber?*
- *a pub landlord?*
- *a member of staff at your bank – face to face, also by phone?*
- *staff selling tickets at a cinema or theatre – face to face, also by phone?*
- *a receptionist at a leisure centre or hotel – face to face, also by phone?*
- *a person on the phone wanting to sell you double glazing?*

On some days you will need to speak to people who you may never meet again, and who you might not really want to talk to, or worry about speaking to, but who deserve your respect and attention. If you avoid any kind of communication it can look rude. If you can overcome your worries and the exchange of words goes well, you may consequently come away feeling that you have added to your own, and perhaps their, sense of well-being during the day. A smile and a pleasant greeting help almost any quick word with someone, and often this is all that is needed.

Brief conversations at shop checkouts and so on can be regarded as 'transactional exchanges' that have a script-like formula. For example, at the supermarket checkout a typical exchange might run like this:

Checkout staff: "Hello, would you like some help packing?" or "Hello, would you like a bag?"

The customer has perhaps three option types: "Hello, no thanks" or "Hello, no I think I'm fine with packing thanks", or "Hello, yes please, I'd like a bag, I left all mine at home."

Using a small amount of eye contact and a smile will make you come across at the right level of friendliness, especially if you add a "Thank you" at the end of the transaction. Thank yous are important in any setting, by the way. Don't miss an opportunity to offer your thanks.

A few extra notes

Sometimes there is a problem with the skills or mood of the other person – the shop assistant might be feeling unhappy that day, for example, so don't be downhearted if you don't get much of a response.

Special cases

There are some occasions when it is important to have a clear plan of what you want to say before you speak. This is especially true of a visit to the doctor or dentist. People often respond to the doctor's question "How are you?" with an automatic "I'm fine, thanks" – the response normally used in everyday chat. However, in this setting we need to be able to give our symptoms clearly and concisely (most doctors allow about five minutes for the whole consultation). It can be useful to have your symptoms written down to refer to, so that you don't miss anything out. Show this list to the doctor if you don't want to tell him.

It's also a good idea, if you have more than one problem, to mention this at the start. You could say: "I have two problems, one is an ingrowing toenail and the other is my bad back." The doctor will then choose which symptom he wants to address first.

At the dentist's all main issues about your teeth need to be asked and answered before he starts work, and as with the doctor, it's best to have prepared a list of your symptoms. The extra problem with dentists is that they have a habit of asking you a question while your mouth is wide open and full of dentistry tools! An answer is impossible in this case; your best bet will be just to grunt and try to smile at the end, on your way out, if your face is not too numb! Raise your hand and make eye contact if there is something important to your treatment while he is actually working on your teeth.

FORMULAIC INTERCHANGES

Try these exercises

- **Observations of Actors**
  Some radio and TV 'soaps' include formulaic interchanges set in pubs or shops. Try to find and record one or two such scenes and then in the group show them, and discuss each 'customer's' and 'trader's' greeting style, the words spoken and the length of the interchange. You could also consider their eye contact and facial expression, and the effect that all of those have on the characters.

- **Observations of Real Life**
  You may observe examples of formulaic interchanges as you go shopping, especially if you have to stand in a supermarket queue. In this case try to remember and afterwards note down anything you have noticed about the interchanges between customers and shop assistants. Regard the queue as a wonderful opportunity to observe!

- **Role Plays**
  In your one-to-one session, or in your group, take turns to practise as many formulaic interchange scenarios as you can, using the types of people at the start of this chapter. You need to try being the trader as well as the customer. It may help the process if you set up the room to suit the scenario, for example, a table partly across a corner of the room to become the bar at a pub or a chair facing a mirror to simulate a hairdresser's.

Formulaic interchanges 'credit cards' for homework

> Today I'm going to try to observe a 'formulaic exchange' on the TV or radio. I'll think about the exchange length and what was said, and retell what I observed in the SLT session.

> Today I'm going to listen to two other people exchanging brief words at the supermarket checkout. I'll think about the exchange length and what was said. I'll retell what I observed in the SLT session.

> Today I'm going to try to have a brief formulaic exchange at a supermarket till. I'll retell what happened at the next SLT session.

> Today I'm going to try to have a brief formulaic exchange at a pub or café. I'll retell what happened at the next SLT session.

> Today I'm going to try phoning the local theatre to ask about performance times for the next production. I'll retell what happened at the next SLT session.

> Today I'm going to try to have a brief formulaic exchange with any one of the following: a hairdresser/barber; a waiter; a member of staff at my bank (face to face or by phone); a person selling a magazine on the street.

FORMAL AND CASUAL CONVERSATIONS

Self-assessment questionnaire

On a scale of 1–10, where 1 is difficult and 10 is easy, how do you feel about recognising the differences between formal and casual conversation settings, and being able to use the right 'code' in the following situations:

- *a barbecue party?*
- *a wedding?*
- *an interview?*
- *a fancy-dress party?*
- *a law court?*
- *a visit to the doctor?*
- *a visit to an elderly relative in hospital?*
- *a day out to a theme park?*
- *an open day at a college?*
- *a ceremony?*
- *a caution by the police?*
- *a chat with your sister's children?*

For many people several of the above settings are unlikely to be encountered. However, this chapter is a basis for discussing the best ways to speak and act should the need arise, even in situations that are either more formal or more casual than usual, and out of our comfort zone.

For some people the formal conversational style of a ceremony or interview when you have well-prepared questions will be easier than the less clearly defined chat needed for casual settings. For others the casual chat is much easier than the formality of special occasions.

Try these exercises

- **Images**

    Find photos in newspapers of different social settings, such as those mentioned in this chapter's questionnaire. Try to find photos of things like royal occasions, local school sports days, family holidays and court proceedings.

    Sort and grade them from the most casual to the most formal settings, and stick them onto a large sheet of paper or card, with the most formal items arranged across the top, the most casual at the bottom and the others graded in between.

    Use sticky notes in the shape of speech bubbles; write on them the types of greetings and conversation topics that the people might use.

    Also discuss what the people are wearing and where else they might wear those clothes.

- **Discussion**

    Discuss these words/terms: posh, snobby, scruffy, classy, casual, formal, smart-casual, social code.

- **Greetings**

    Rate these greeting types in terms of their degree of formality:

    - Spoken versions, including: "Good morning", "Wassup", "Hi", "Hello", "Watcha", "Morning", "Hiya", "Hi there".

    - Non-verbal versions including: handshake, 'High 5', hearty slap on the shoulder, peck on the cheek, repeated 'pecks on the cheek' by heads of state.

    - Written or email versions including: Dear Sir/Madam, Hi, Dear Mr/Mrs, Darling.

- **Goodbyes**

    Rate these verbal and non-verbal closings in terms of their degree of formality:

    - Spoken versions, including: "Bye", "Cheers", "Farewell", "Goodbye", "See you", "Ciao", "Later/Laters".

    - Non-verbal versions including: handshake, 'High 5', hug.

    - Written or email versions including: Yours sincerely, Yours faithfully, Thanks, Take care, Best wishes, Regards, Cheers, See you.

FORMAL AND CASUAL CONVERSATIONS

- **Topics**

  For further details on topic choice please see the chapter on 'Choosing and introducing a conversation topic'. For now, look at the following topics of conversation and decide which type of occasion they are most suited to, formal occasions/ceremonies, relaxed/casual occasions or appropriate for all situations:

  - *the weather*
  - *current events*
  - *your own health*
  - *your child's temper tantrums*
  - *your girlfriend or boyfriend*
  - *politics*
  - *jokes*
  - *art*
  - *what you saw on TV last night*
  - *'green' issues*
  - *the occasion you are attending.*

- **Role Play**

  Describe and then role play the way you would enter the room/building on arrival at the following occasions and what your first words might be:

  - *a noisy party*
  - *a wedding*
  - *an interview*
  - *a family reunion*
  - *a school reunion after five years of leaving the school*
  - *a funeral*
  - *your own house when everyone is already watching a really good TV programme.*

The Conversation Strategies Manual

Formal and casual conversations 'credit cards' for homework

> Today I'm going to try to find photos of myself at any formal occasions I've attended. What did I wear? What sort of things did I talk about? How did I feel?

> Today I'm going to try to find some photos of myself at a party or sports event. What did I wear? What sort of things did I talk about? How did I feel?

> Today I'm going to say hello in an appropriately casual way to three people.

> Today I'm going to try to find appropriate opportunities to greet three people in a formal way.

> Today I'm going to sit in a café and try to notice three people dressed casually and three dressed formally.

> Today I'll consider any social events coming up for me. I'll rate them on a formal/casual scale. At the next SLT session I'll discuss my ideas for clothing, greeting style and conversation topics for those events.

BODY LANGUAGE

10

The term 'body language' encompasses many aspects of the way we communicate and can be thought of in terms of (1) how we express it and (2) how we interpret it in other people, so there are two self-assessment questionnaires for this chapter.

Self-assessment questionnaire on expressing body language

On a scale of 1–10, where 1 is difficult and 10 is easy, how do you feel about these aspects of body language:

- using eye contact with a friend as you greet them?
- using eye contact in a conversation – occasionally when you are the speaker and frequently when you are the listener?
- dividing your eye contact between a group of friends or colleagues?
- smiling broadly as you greet your friend?
- using facial expressions accurately?
- using a faint smile as you greet anyone?
- understanding and using gesture?
- understanding and using posture?
- shaking hands with somebody?

Self-assessment questionnaire on interpreting body language

On a scale of 1–10, how do you feel about interpreting these aspects of body language in others:

- noticing facial movements such as eyebrow position, openness of eyes, degree of smile, lips curling up or down, nose wrinkling, furrowing of forehead as in frowning?
- matching facial expressions to emotions, for example: tears on a person's cheek; blushing; the surprise on the face of a person unexpectedly meeting a friend; shock when someone receives bad news?
- understanding what is being conveyed by a hearty handshake?
- interpreting the emotion felt by a small child stamping his foot?

- *interpreting uncontrollable giggling?*
- *understanding the 'eyes met across a crowded room' scenario?*
- *noticing and understanding: the shoulder shrug; hands on hips; folded arms; a drooping posture?*
- *understanding the meaning of 'personal space'?*
- *understanding what might be conveyed by a person's clothing/fashion choices?*

Some theorists state that as much as 60 per cent, or even more, of our communication is transmitted by body language. Even when important words are spoken, we gain more information through interpreting facial expression, posture and gesture, and we make a point more clearly by adding body language.

Before we even begin to converse with a person we can often see, from the way they walk towards us, from the expression on their face, even from the clothes they wear, how they are feeling. It is worth remembering that you can only make a first impression once. Person A, who enters a room and looks pleased at the prospect of meeting friends, or a new acquaintance, will tend to be more warmly received than Person B, who grandly arrives looking as if they expect others to be somehow grateful for his presence.

Since the inventions of Skype (or similar) and video conferencing, much body language – especially facial expression – has been reintroduced after temporarily losing it to the facelessness of the phone, email and online forum.

Eye contact

Don't be downhearted about a difficulty with this. Some people feel that they ought to look right into the pupil of the other person's eye, but this is not the case. If you watch a TV presenter doing a piece to camera they seem to be looking right at you, but in fact they are usually achieving the same effect by reading from an autocue placed just above the camera lens. In the same way you can achieve the effect of eye contact when in fact you are looking just above, below or between the other person's eyes. You can even avoid the whole problem by looking at the mouth instead of the eyes.

Personal space

It is usually best to err on the side of 'too far away' rather than 'too close' when you are talking with someone and certainly best not to touch a person. A good rule for how close to stand is 'arm's length'. It's important to try to consider how to share space, for example, on a sofa, train or in a waiting room. Aim to be equally spaced so that in a waiting room occupied by just one other person it's best not to sit next to them, but sit across the corner of the room from them instead.

Try these exercises

For eye contact

- **Big Eyes**
  In your one-to-one session, or in your group, someone draws a face with a biggish pair of eyes showing the details of the pupils and irises of the eyes, and the eyelashes, eyebrows, bridge of the nose and the upper cheeks. Discuss the comparative difficulty of looking into the pupils rather than the other areas around the eyes. For those willing, try looking into each other's eyes and then try looking at the surrounding area.

- **Guess What I'm Looking At**
  Place a number of picture cards around the room and each take turns to look at a card while the others try to guess what you are looking at.

- **Eyes Closed**
  Try a short conversation where the listener closes their eyes. How did the speaker feel? Try a conversation where the speaker closes his eyes. How do the listeners feel? Discuss both scenarios.

- **Expressions**
  Discuss these expressions: 'eyeballing'; 'looking shifty'; 'doe-eyed'; 'blanking someone'; 'wide-eyed'; 'look the world in the eye': 'catch someone's eye'.

- **Wink Murder**
  This is only suitable for a group of four or more, in fact the more the better. In case you are unfamiliar with this old game, all you do is the following: (1) Prepare small pieces of paper, one for each person and write M (for murderer) on one and D (for detective) on another, and fold them all up so that the M and the D are hidden. (2) Each person takes one of the pieces of paper, unfolds it but hides it, so that the 'murderer' is secret. The detective will declare their role. (3) All have a longish conversation about anything but during which everyone needs to keep looking at each other. (4) During the conversation the 'murderer' will wink at someone, who immediately feigns death. (5) The detective guesses who the murderer is. If he succeeds, the game is over and you have to start again. If he fails to select the 'criminal' the conversation begins again and the 'murderer' can strike again. This is good fun and the humour lightens the burden of making eye contact.

For facial expression

- **Images**

  Using newspapers, colour supplements and magazines, look for people expressing emotions and, without reading the story in the paper, try to think how they are feeling and discuss some possible reasons.

- **Emotions**

  In your one-to-one session, or in your group, consider the following emotions:

  - *happy, sad, excited, disgusted, surprised, tired, depressed, proud, bored, in pain, annoyed, giggly, shocked, interested, disapproving, etc.*

  Practise, preferably with a mirror, making the facial expressions that go with these emotions. Discuss some of the emotions and decide for each example:

  - *what makes me feel …? What might make other people feel …?*

  - *what might I say when I feel …? What might other people say when they feel …?*

  - *what does my body do when I feel …? What do other people's bodies do when they feel …?*

  - *how do I sound when I feel …? How do other people sound when they feel …?*

  - *what helps me when I feel …? What might help other people when they feel …?*

  - *are there times when we should not look …?*

- **Mirror**

  Again in a mirror, practise smiling, and observe and discuss the different effects to be gained from (a) a quick smile on an otherwise unmoving face, and (b) a wide smile which is slow to fade, and has some wrinkling up of the corners of the eyes. Is an immediate smile best or a smile which grows once you have fully taken in the recipient of it?

  Try the 'Smile/Scowl' contest. In pairs, look at each other. One makes a tight, angry scowling face. The other keeps looking at the 'scowler' but smiles. The scowler tends, usually, to loosen their angry face eventually and start to look more pleasant. See how long this takes; time it.

For posture and gesture

- **Non-Verbal Greetings**
  Try out as many different non-verbal greetings as you can think of (do this around the circle if you are in a group).

- **Posture Barriers**
  Discuss the term 'posture barriers'. These postures – folded arms, hugging of clipboard or book, perhaps crossing their legs, turning slightly away so that the back or shoulder forms a barrier – are often referred to as 'closed postures' and may indicate that a person is not feeling as if they want to talk. (Although it has to be said that sometimes people fold their arms when they are feeling cold!)

  Arms unfolded, maybe arm outstretched along the back of a chair and facing the conversation partner, are 'open postures'. Try these postures out on each other. Extend the effect of the open posture by making sure your whole body, not just your eyes, swivels to face the conversation partner.

- **Posture in Motion**
  Each person in the group in turn goes out and then re-enters the room in one of two ways, (1) slouching, drooping, shuffling their feet, and (2) standing up straight and moving more smoothly, then repeats the exercise entering the room in the other way. The rest of the group discuss which posture looks more confident and which more shy. Note: the group leader may need to demonstrate the ways of entering the room.

- **Mirroring**
  Discuss the term 'mirroring'. Watch part of a TV 'soap' where two people are supposed to be in love, also watch part of a discussion programme, perhaps a show where they are reviewing the arts or discussing sport. See how often the actors or participants mirror, or partially mirror, each other's gestures and postures: do they both touch their hair, cross their legs or lean back at roughly the same time? In a conversation between two people in your group, try mirroring each other's body language as you talk and then try it without mirroring. How do the effects differ?

- **True or False**
  Try making a true and then a false statement to each other using an 'honest' open posture, with shoulders tilted slightly forward, arms slightly apart and palms up. Also try out and then discuss what happens if you make a statement and touch your face, cross and uncross your legs or otherwise fidget. It's usually best to avoid fidgeting while you speak or listen.

- **Clothes**

    Find pictures in fashion magazines (men's and women's) and in newspapers. Aim to get pictures showing people of different types – goths, business people, smartly dressed people, less tidy people, people in uniform, people at a wedding, others playing sports or attending a sports event (painted football faces included!) and so on. Discuss what we can tell about people by their clothes and the effect that wearing different types of clothes has on us.

- **Charades**

    Play a game of charades. Enjoy the miming and discuss how many of these mimes we use in our everyday talking.

- **Set Your Distance**

    Try having a chat with another member of the group, firstly when you are much too close, then too far away (so that you have to speak too loudly). How do you, and they, feel?

- **Perfume**

    Discuss in the group the effects of smell, another aspect of body language. For some people the scent of perfume or deodorant can be overpowering so there's a need to use products judiciously or use a perfume-free deodorant. Most people prefer to have a definite hint of a pleasant smell coming from others. Pleasant smells tend to indicate cleanliness and a sense that a person takes care of themselves.

BODY LANGUAGE

Body language 'credit cards' for homework

> Today I'm going to try making fleeting eye contact with six people.

> Today I'll experiment with eye contact according to what I need to practise. This could be practice in just looking once towards the eye area of a conversation partner but not directly into the pupils or looking at them while they are speaking.

> Today I'm going to try to 'catch someone's eye' when I need to speak to them. This could be catching the eye of the waiter/waitress in a café.

> Today I'm going to watch a TV conversation and look out for signs of 'mirroring' of body language. I'll also look for any posture barriers.

> Today I'm going to observe how close to each other most people tend to stand when they are having a conversation. I'll make sure I stand at arm's length for a conversation.

> Today I'll watch people in a café or canteen. I'll especially look out for friends meeting there and how soon they make eye contact as they become aware of each other's presence. I'll recount what I saw when I'm in the next SLT session.

51

WHAT ARE OTHER PEOPLE'S INTERESTS?

Self-assessment questionnaire

On a scale of 1–10, where 1 is difficult and 10 is easy, how do you feel about discovering your conversation partner's interests, when the person in question is:

- *a friend of the same sex as you?*
- *a friend of the opposite sex?*
- *a new acquaintance?*
- *a potential new girlfriend/boyfriend?*

This short section adds to the next two chapters about asking questions, 'Open and closed questions and invitations to speak' and 'The www. technique', which all provide contributions to the content of a conversation. Please also see the chapter 'Choosing and introducing a conversation topic'.

I'm talking about social skills here, rather than detective work, but there are a few occasions when you might need to find out about a person without actually asking them directly:

- Suppose you have made a friend and have talked with them quite a lot, but you are going to an occasion where you will need to introduce that person to someone else. You want to be able to say a few words about their interests to 'connect' them with the other person. How can you work out what to say?

- Suppose you have known a person for years, but haven't really noticed which activities they actually like. How could you plan a surprise party for them?

- Suppose you want to buy a present for your friend, but despite your previous conversations you are not really sure what would be the type of gift that he or she would like to receive. How could you find out?

- Suppose you have been invited to go to a concert/film/outing and to bring a friend, but are not quite sure which of your friends to ask to go with you. How can you go about making a decision?

One approach to these sorts of problems is to make use of the information-gathering potential of moments in a conversation when something is mentioned; it could be a trip to some caves, a sporting event, a wish to visit a particular town, a wish to own something that someone else has and so on, which will give you clues to that person's interests. It's good to jot these ideas down after the conversation if you have trouble remembering details.

Another solution is to talk to a mutual friend or relative of theirs. If you do this you'll need to plan the questions beforehand and take a notebook to write down their suggestions.

Another plan is to consider things in the person's house, if you are fortunate enough to be invited there. Take a close look – are there lots of books about magic/fishing/music of a particular period? Are there any sports trophies? Are there lots of CDs and so on by a particular musician/singer? Are there any collections of keys/clocks/train timetables and so on? These could all be clues about a person's interests and dreams. You will, of course, have to make sure that such items are theirs and don't belong to a different family member or to their flatmate!

Try these exercises

- **Desert Island Gifts**
  Listen to or watch recordings of radio or TV interviews. 'Desert Island Discs' on Radio 4 is a great starting point. From what is said on the programme, discuss what might be a good idea for a gift that the celebrity would like to receive – for their ordinary life, not for the desert island! That would be too easy.

- **Star Topics**
  Find photos in newspapers of celebrities or people who have achieved something (could be an award, a trophy, a medal). If you could meet that person what three topics do you think they would like to talk about?

- **The Interview Game**
  In pairs interview another person in the group, with the aim of finding out three or more useful facts about him or her, but without actually asking directly. You can ask the person to tell you about their childhood, what they like doing and their last holiday. Take five minutes for this. Then take three minutes to make a note of ideas for a conversation topic, a gift, a day out and something else interesting that you could mention when introducing them to someone else. Then reverse roles so that you become the interviewee. When everyone has interviewed another person and been interviewed, report your findings back to the group.

What are other people's interests? 'credit cards' for homework

> Today I'm going to listen to an interview on a radio programme. I'll make a note of the programme and the interviewee, and think of an idea for a gift for that person, then report all this back to the group.

> Today I'll watch a TV interview. I'll make a note of the programme and the interviewee, and some interesting facts about them that I'd mention if I were to introduce the person to someone else who I know. I'll report all this back to the group.

> Today I'll listen to or watch an interview on radio or TV, and note any interesting facts about the interviewee. Who would make a good conversational pairing with that person? (It could be another famous person.) I'll report back to the group.

> Today I'm going to think of five people who I send Christmas cards to. What details about myself would each person like to hear about? Which of my interests match theirs?

> Today I am collecting my friend to go somewhere. I'll arrive slightly early and while my friend is getting ready I'll ask their flatmate/parent/sibling if they have any ideas about what my friend would like for their birthday.

> Today I'm going to my friend's house for supper. While they are out of the room I'll take a look at their books or CDs, look at the pictures on their walls, and see if I can find out any clues about interests they have that I didn't already know about.

OPEN AND CLOSED QUESTIONS AND INVITATIONS TO SPEAK

Self-assessment questionnaire

On a scale of 1–10, where 1 is difficult and 10 is easy, how do you feel about asking social questions in a conversation with the following types of people:

- a member of your family?
- a friend?
- a new person?
- a prospective girlfriend/boyfriend?
- a group of friends?

In some conversations you may feel as if you need a way to promote or prolong the other person's comments, because you seem to be doing all the work of keeping things going. One way to do this is to ask questions that require more than a one-word answer, and the skill is just to take on board the concept of open and closed questions.

A *closed* question is one where your conversation partner can answer with a response of one word or a short phrase. This form of question can be useful, but sometimes it causes the conversation to come to a halt.

For example, if you ask: "Did you like the film?" your conversation partner only needs to reply, "Yes" or "No".

Similarly, if you ask: "Where did you go on holiday?" the response need only be, "To France". Too many questions like this will make you sound like an inquisitor rather than a conversationalist and it will be hard work for you to keep things going.

Closed questions can also start with a short statement followed by a tag question, for example: "Eggs are expensive, aren't they?", "Her case looked heavy, didn't it?" They still invite one-word or very short answers.

An *open* question is one where your respondent will need to remember or reflect, and give a shortish narrative or an opinion. You might ask: "What did you do at the weekend?" which can draw out a longer response than the closed question: "Did you have a nice weekend?"

Similarly if you ask: "How did you get on at the interview?" you should get a much fuller answer than you will from: "Did you get the job?"

Connected to the open question is the *'invitation to speak'* that is not actually a question as such, for example: "I'd love to hear about your holiday in France" or "I wonder why he was running so fast?" If you accompany this with an interested, expectant look it invites your respondent to give you a short narrative or opinion in the same way as an open question does.

Often one or even two *closed* questions can form a good starting point, to establish the context, and will be followed by an open question, for example: "Did you go to see that film you mentioned?" (closed question) to which they might say: "Yes", which you can then follow up with: "What did you think about it?" (open question). This provides the opportunity for them to tell you their feelings about the film in a way that: "Did you like that film you went to see?" might not.

If you have now succeeded in getting a conversation started, you can capitalise on your effort, and keep things going by asking careful questions here and there within the general conversation.

Ben: *Hi Jerry!*

Ben: *Hello Ben*

Ben: *Had a good holiday?* (Closed question)

Ben: *Yes, thanks.*

Ben: *Where was it that you went?* (Closed question)

Ben: *Tenerife*

Ben: *What did you think of it?* (Open question)

Ben: *I really liked it, there was so much to see around the coast and up in the hills, and there was lots to do.*

Ben: *What sorts of things did you do?* (Open question)

Ben: *I swam a lot, and went on boat rides to the other islands.*

Ben: *That sounds good. I'd love to hear your recommendations for hotels for people like me on a budget.* (Invitation to speak)

And Jerry answers with some detail.

Try these exercises

- **Discussion**
  In your one-to-one session, or in your group, discuss the theory and usefulness of open and closed questions, and talk about how often they are used.

- **Halting and Flowing Interviews**
  Discuss radio or TV interviews that keep grinding to a halt, and those that seem to flow. Interviews between an inexperienced TV presenter and a child often contain far too many closed questions, and almost no open questions or invitations to speak, so that the whole of their conversation sounds stilted and awkward. Try to record a few interviews like this, with a presenter and an unforthcoming interviewee, and consider together how the interview could be improved.

- **Question Circle**
  Try a circle game involving hypothetical open and closed questions in a group setting. The first person in the circle will ask a closed question such as: "Do you like plane journeys?", the next will reply, "Yes" or "No"; the next will invite a response, for example: "Tell me about your first memory of flying", so the next will describe a journey made as a child (this might involve getting lost at the airport or loving the view, hating the food, liking the film etc), the next person will ask a closed question, for example: "Would you take a small child on a plane journey?" the next will say, "Yes" or "No", the next asks an open question: "What do you think are the best ways to entertain a small child on a journey?"… and so it goes on, one closed question, one open question or invitation to speak, one closed question, one open question or invitation to speak.

- **Role Play**
  Role play lots of open and closed questions in scenarios similar to the Ben and Jerry example. The acted scenarios could be conversations with:

  - *a colleague at coffee break at work*
  - *your teenage son*
  - *a social evening with a friend you haven't seen for a year*
  - *a phone call with a new girlfriend/boyfriend.*

- **Tag**

    Remember the closed question or statement with tag? Try this exercise as a group. Each think up and then all discuss closed questions, statements with tags and follow-up open questions or invitations to speak, about each of the following themes:

    Gardening   *Sport*

    Nightclubs   *TV*

    Work   *A current event*

    Travel   *Theatre*

Open and closed questions and invitations to speak 'credit cards' for homework

> Today I'll listen to a radio or TV interview and listen out specifically for moments in the interview where the interviewer failed to use enough open questions, and things went awkwardly. I'll make notes and report back to the SLT session.

> Today I'll listen to a radio or TV interview and notice the atmosphere changing when good questions extended the conversation. If I can record this I will bring it to the session next time. Otherwise I'll make notes and report back to the session.

> Today I'm going to try out a closed then an open question in a conversation at home with a member of my family.

> Today I'm going to try out a closed then an open question, then an invitation to speak, in a conversation with a friend.

> Today I'm going to try out a closed then an open question in a conversation at work.

> Today I'm going to try out a closed then an open question in a telephone conversation.

THE WWW. TECHNIQUE

13

Self-assessment questionnaire

On a scale of 1–10, where 1 is difficult and 10 is easy, how do you feel about keeping a conversation going with:

- *just one friend?*
- *a group of friends?*
- *a new person?*

By now you may have tackled several aspects of conversation, found your confidence in discovering people's interests, and feel happy about the difference between open and closed questions.

This chapter aims to help you to find a very easy way to extend conversations even further.

What does the term www. make you think of? As part of our IT lives maybe it makes us think of extending our knowledge into a wide perspective and in conversational terms it helps us to widen the scope of the chat.

In this case www. stands for Who? Where? and Why? The dot reminds us to dot about between these 'W' questions. These can be added within the conversation at the appropriate time.

'Who?' questions apply to a number of things to do with people. They do not actually have to begin with the word 'Who' – for example, if the topic is about a trip to a shopping centre the 'who' questions could be: "Was it crowded?" or "Are the staff there helpful?" but could also include: "Who did you go with?" and so on, so all these questions are connected with one or more people.

'Where?' is anything to do with the location: "Have they repainted the swimming pool changing rooms yet?" or "Is the theatre's air conditioning working now?" and so on, so again the questions do not have to begin with the word 'Where' but only need to relate to the venue.

'Why?' is connected with the purpose of the visit: "Is that part of your keep-fit programme?", "Was it a special trip to that town or were you on the way home?" and so on.

These types of questions will keep a conversation rolling on, but do be aware that no one likes an inquisition! Remember to be sensitive to the fact that they might want to ask you a question at some point! Reserve the www. technique for when things go a bit quiet.

Once you have started a conversation, that is, the greetings are done and, maybe, followed by an opening gambit, you can ask a closed question, an open question, and then three or more of a mix of www. questions and open/closed questions. The encounter would go something like this (and we're considering *Richard's* talk):

Richard: *Hi Liz!*

Liz: *Hello Richard.*

Richard: *Did you have a good weekend?* (Closed question)

Liz: *Yes, thanks, and you?*

Richard: *Yes, mine was fine thanks. What did you do?* (Open question)

Liz: *I went to the Leisure Centre for the afternoon, it was really nice there.*

Richard: *Did you take your children this time or did you manage to get some time to yourself?* ('Who?' question).

Liz: *I took my daughter, but my sons went to football practice.*

Richard: *That's nice. Where did you park?* ('Where?' question)

Liz: *I was lucky and found a parking place there easily.*

Richard: *That's good, parking around there can be tricky. Do you do any sports yourself?* (Closed question which, with rising intonation, invites an expanded answer)

Liz: *Yes, I'm trying to do an hour's running every day and if I get good enough I'm hoping to build up to even more.*

Richard: *That's impressive! Is it for your own fitness or are you aiming to compete?* (The 'Why?' is implied)

Liz: *Well, if I get good enough I'm hoping to do a half-marathon.*

You can of course add 'What?' and 'When?' along with 'How?' to your list of question types.

Try these exercises

- **Discuss**

  In your one-to-one session, or in your group, discuss the theory and usefulness of the www. techniques, for example, how would you use them without sounding as if this is a formula that you've learned? (Even though it is!)

- **Question Dice**

  Make a 'Question Dice' (please see Appendix 2) and use it to practise asking not only the main www. questions, but the others too. Roll the dice and ask your neighbour a question starting with that word.

- **Scenarios**

  Act out some www. scenarios, similar to the Liz and Richard sample above. The scenarios could be conversations with:

  - *a colleague at coffee break at work*
  - *a social evening with friends you see often*
  - *a social evening with a friend you haven't seen for a year*
  - *the waiting area at a company where you are going for an interview for a job*
  - *a phone call with a new girlfriend/boyfriend*
  - *the social meeting time after a funeral (a 'wake').*

The www.technique 'credit cards' for homework

Today I'm going to listen to a radio or TV 'soap', make a note of any www. techniques used and report back to the SLT session.	Today I'm going to listen to a radio or TV interview, make a note of any www. techniques used and report back to the SLT session.
Today I'm going to try out the www. techniques in a conversation at home with a member of my family.	Today I'm going to try out the www. techniques in a conversation with a friend.
Today I'm going to try out the www. techniques in a conversation at work.	Today I'm going to try out the www. techniques in a telephone conversation.

CHOOSING AND INTRODUCING A CONVERSATION TOPIC 14

Self-assessment questionnaire

On a scale of 1–10, where 1 is difficult and 10 is easy, how do you feel about choosing and introducing a topic with:

- *just one friend?*

- *a mixed group of friends in a casual setting?*

- *people from your workplace in a formal setting?*

In any conversation a useful topic to talk about will be whatever the other speaker is mentioning at the time, and the key here is to *listen to them carefully* and try to extend their point by making a comment of your own about the same subject. However, have you ever been in a conversation that has become awkwardly quiet and worried that you will not be able to think of anything to say?

This happens from time to time with most people and largely depends on the expectations of each of the speakers; some are very happy with what they see as a 'comfortable silence' while others see every silence as uncomfortable.

If you are worried about how to deal with conversational gaps one approach is to collect and remember ideas for any conversation that might occur, and to prepare for a particular conversation that you know you will be having that day, by having some potential topics 'up your sleeve'. However, you don't need to have a 'set piece' that you have rehearsed – this will sound artificial and will be difficult to insert into the conversation.

In general it's a good idea to relate the topic to the person's interests, so if you are chatting to someone you know to be a florist or a farmer, try to connect some of your comments to those subjects, but don't restrict the conversation to that, after all, they may want to talk about *your* job or interests!

The weather and people's journeys are often very useful topics; they will be appropriate for nearly every type of person you meet. Another useful topic, if conversation seems to be flagging a bit, is to mention food in some way – either a recent delicious meal that you have enjoyed or ask them if they can recommend any food shops, recipes or cafés.

Choosing a variety of topics becomes easier if you have in mind a little verse used by brides when deciding what to wear on their wedding day. The original verse goes like this:

Something old (perhaps a piece of jewellery passed down from a grandmother)

Something new (the wedding dress itself)

Something borrowed (perhaps the veil)

Something blue (often a blue garter or an inconspicuous blue ribbon).

For selecting topics of conversation the verse can be used like this:

Something old – a recap of elements of a previous conversation you have had with this person, for example: "How did you get on with the search for your new car?" or "How was your weekend in London?", or "How is your sister, is she any better?" (This is where it might have been helpful to have made a note of anything significant that they said at your last chat with them.)

Something new – something from the news on TV/radio/the newspapers. Are you, or could you become, a bit up to date with the latest news? The headlines, and one or two other stories, preferably one with a humorous angle to it, are good beginnings. "Did you see that story on the TV news about that little girl who won a medal for bravery?" or "Did you see in the local paper that they are planning to build a new shopping centre right out of town?" or "I heard on the news that Arsenal are doing well again now that they've bought that new player". Ask if they also heard or saw that item on radio or TV news or read about it. Listen to what they think about the story and give your own opinion, but try not to be controversial.

Something borrowed – an item about a radio or TV programme or film, that is, not your own news, but that of the familiar characters, for example: "Have you seen the new *Mission Impossible* film? That was a scary car chase wasn't it?", "Did you see *Eastenders*? What did you think about …?" (Take care to 'match your soaps' though, because they might never have watched your favourite 'soap' or might not watch them at all.)

Something blue – some news of yours to which you have an emotional response; these remarks often contain the words: "I feel …" The emotion will be anything from happy, to surprised, to gloomy, shocked and so on (but take care to avoid overloading your conversation partner with your problems).

CHOOSING AND INTRODUCING A CONVERSATION TOPIC

Are there any 'taboo' topics to avoid?

Money, religion and politics were once considered to be topics to be avoided in polite conversation. Nowadays these can usually be discussed, but be careful not to polarise opinion. Remember that people will have different ideas, be relatively richer or poorer than others, or belong to a different religion and may be embarrassed to find themselves isolated.

Most subjects are fine, but take care with the subjects of sex and death, both of which may be awkward for some. My advice is not to mention a subject if you are unsure whether it would be taboo for this conversation partner.

Introducing a new topic

It can be confusing when conversations flit about from one topic to another. To quote from a young man I used to work with: "People seem to be adding random topics." Sometimes it is difficult to keep pace with conversations like that and if we ourselves tend to change the topic unexpectedly we can make matters worse. The key is to listen carefully and focus on the main topic that your conversation partner/partners is talking about. Your comments should follow on naturally from what they are saying. If you have something relevant to add, then add it at a good moment when there is a gap. So, if they are talking about a film recently seen, try to add a comment about that film if you saw it too, or mention another film that had a similar theme or the same lead actor in it.

In a good conversation one idea will naturally emerge from another, so that a chat about someone's new car might segue into a completely different topic via: the garage where they bought the car; the road where that garage is situated; the pub in that road; what the food is like in that pub; another pub where you went with your family for a meal; and finally into a chat about food in general. Many conversations are like that, rolling along in an unplanned way, covering seemingly disconnected topics, but joined in a fluid way. If you listen to a radio or TV 'magazine' programme you may notice the great efforts made to create the 'seamless link'. For example, I recently heard an item about public participation in counting birds in their garden; the next item was to be about a jewellery theft, so the presenter's link between the topics was to mention the magpies in his garden, the habit of magpies to steal shiny things, such as milk bottle tops and jewellery ... a neat lead-in to the jewellery theft item!

Rapid changes of conversation topic will seem disjointed and will make the conversation partner feel that you have not been listening. Try to stay on a topic until you feel it has become exhausted. Then you can start a new topic of conversation.

Probably the most common general topic to talk about, after the weather and their journey, is the person's occupation; this usually refers to a job or a stage in their education. With a new acquaintance you can ask what they do and follow this with some questions about their job, possibly linking some aspect of it to your own occupation. With friends, you will already know what their job is, but you could ask about how it's going.

It is possible to engineer the conversation so that you can talk about something that you have chosen. However, sometimes you will need to prepare the other speaker by using a 'topic-shifting statement'. Please see 'Try these exercises', 'Topic shifting' below, for further clarification on this point.

It is sometimes possible, in a lengthy conversation where participants are good friends in a playful mood, to use a kind of fantasy quiz game as a topic. These types of questions could begin the chat: "If you won £3 million (or any amount) what would you do with it?", "If you could travel forwards or backwards in time which time would you go for and why?", "If you could have a celebrity here with us who would it be?", "If you could have a superpower what would it be?" There are potential conversation topics of this kind in some table trivia games.

The benefits of this kind of topic are that you will be able to extend the conversation, find out a little more about this person and be able to differ in your ideas in an entirely non-argumentative way. After all, what does it matter if you would like to meet Shakespeare while they would like it to be Lord Sugar? Again, the tricky part is to shoehorn the game into the conversation in a natural way so, for example, if the conversation turns to comments about money, that might be the moment to ask what they would do if they won the lottery. If you are talking about somebody famous, there's a cue for asking which celebrity they would choose to have present in the room.

Try these exercises

- **What the Papers Say**
  Have a look at a few newspapers and find possible topics of conversation. In a group therapy session you can each summarise an article for discussion.

- **Film Reviews**
  Bring along a leaflet from your local cinema, discuss the films, decide on the genre of each and talk about what kind of people might enjoy that film. If you were going to see it who might you invite to go along and see it with you?

- **Topic and Person Matching**
  Each think of a type of person and think of two things they might like to talk about, and two things that might not be appropriate. Here are some person types to help you get started:

  - *an elderly aunt who used to work in a sweetshop*
  - *an uncle who was a teacher*
  - *a hairdresser*
  - *a sportsperson*
  - *a student studying English/art/maths*
  - *a musician.*

- **Topic Shifting**
  Topic shifting statements are phrases like: "On a similar topic …"; "Oh, that reminds me of another occasion …"; "Sorry to change the subject completely"; "I know this is butterflying about a bit but …"; "On a completely different subject …" or "Apropos of nothing at all …" If you have a large blank cube/dice you could write one of these statements on each side, to form a 'topic-shifting dice'.

  Have a list of conversation topics written on cards (in words or pictures) handy, placed face down on the table. One group member turns a card over and begins a conversation with another about that topic. At any moment the therapist will roll the topic-shifting dice or just turn over another card with a different topic and show it to a member of the group. Using a topic-shifting statement such as the above, the next person has to bring in that new topic. See how long the group can keep this going. Discuss how it felt to be the person bringing in the new topic and how it felt for the rest of the group.

- Further ideas for conversation topics are mentioned in other chapters such as 'What are other people's interests?', 'Noticing, commenting and making polite observations' and 'Reminiscing and reflecting'.

Choosing and introducing a conversation topic 'credit cards' for homework

> Today I'm going to read the local paper and make a note of a funny or interesting story. Later I'll mention this story to someone at work. I'll also bring the article back to the group for discussion.

> Today I'll read 'gossip' about four people – politicians, celebrities, sportspeople – and consider conversation topics, apart from their main job, that might interest them. I'll discuss the articles and my ideas back in the group.

> Today I'm going to try, in a chat with my neighbour or someone at work, to recap part of a previous conversation I had with them, so forming a renewed topic of conversation.

> Today I'm going to try mentioning a particular storyline of a TV 'soap' to a friend who is also keen on the same programme.

> Today, at a relaxed, casual social event with friends I'm going to try to introduce a 'fantasy' topic at a good moment. Maybe it will be: "If you won the lottery what would you do with the money?"

> Today in a phone call with a friend I'll bring into the conversation a film I have seen recently at the cinema. I'll either join this to a comment my friend makes or I'll use a topic-shifting device.

NOTICING, COMMENTING AND MAKING POLITE OBSERVATIONS

15

Self-assessment questionnaire

On a scale of 1–10, where 1 is difficult and 10 is easy, how do you feel about noticing and commenting, that is, observing your surroundings or other people and making comments about them in the following types of situation:

- a hotel, café, restaurant or pub?
- a stately home, park or garden open to the public?
- a religious building, museum or art gallery?
- the high street in your local town?
- a friend's house or garden?
- a hospital?
- a university or college open day?
- a barbecue party or a fancy-dress party?

This chapter looks at how we can make use of our surroundings and the people we notice as 'talking points' when a conversation is flagging or if it fails to get going.

A comment about the area, the building or the decorative surroundings may reinvigorate things. Items inviting comment might be the low ceiling of an ancient pub or its large fireplace. I know a pub where there are tables and chairs, and even beer mats and glasses all somehow stuck to the ceiling; that's a feature worth a comment. Perhaps a talking point is the fantastic view from the window of a stately home open to the public, or an attractive lake or beautiful tree in a park. In a town, try looking above the shop fronts to the upper storeys of the original buildings where there might be some interesting architecture to comment about.

It used to be said that we should never make personal comments, however, a positive comment about your conversation partner could form a compliment in addition to extending the conversation. You could mention that you like their interesting scarf or brooch, for example, which might draw out a comment from them about where it came from. You could also try making polite observations about your conversation partner, for example: "You like sitting by the window don't you?" or "I've noticed you tend to go for salads rather than stews." Again you are likely to bring about a response which might begin a new topic.

An observation about other people could enhance and add humour to the conversation as long as the people are not too close and your comment is not impolite. Try sitting at a table outside a café in the summer – it is almost impossible not to make comments about passers-by! Plenty of conversation fuel can come from such observations.

On a car or train journey there will be plenty of things to see and comment about: funny names of streets or villages, beautiful gardens, murals and graffiti. You might see people out jogging, riding, knocking at a door, walking their dog. All these could be worthy of a comment and might begin a new strand in the conversation.

Try these exercises

- **Venues**

    Everyone in the group should look for photos of different social venues, such as those mentioned in the self-assessment questionnaire at the start of this chapter. Try to find photos of the interiors of these places as well as the outside settings. You'll find suitable photos in leaflets provided by some hotels, pubs, universities, colleges, religious buildings and stately homes open to the public and so on. It doesn't matter if these are years out of date, they are just for practice in noticing things to talk about. You may also find good pictures in newspapers, colour supplements and magazines.

    Take it in turns to practise forming comments about the photos. Some will start with an exclamation such as "Wow!" followed by a question: "Have you noticed the view from here?" Or you might set your comment in context: "This pub is really old isn't it? Have you noticed the date over the fireplace?" or a straight comment such as: "I like that picture in the hallway, there's such a lot of detail in it." Or it could be a less positive comment like: "It's so difficult to park here isn't it?" Of course you can almost always make a comment about the weather.

    Now try to think of non-visual details to use as a basis for comments. Imagine the steam in a little café on a rainy day; the coolness of a cathedral and the sounds of the choir. Role play making comments about those.

    Once you have got the hang of making such comments you will need to practise responding to them. It's best not to leave someone's comment unanswered; it sounds impolite or as if you haven't heard, besides which you might as well make use of their comment to extend the conversation. In general it is a good idea to take a short moment to look at the thing they are commenting about, agree with it, and try to take it a little further, for example:

- A: "What an interesting museum!"
- B: "Yes, it has masses of things to see."

This could then be extended to something like:

- A: "There's almost too much to see in one afternoon."
- B: "Yes, we certainly won't be bored!"

In the group form a 'Comment circle' where one participant looks at a photo and makes a comment, the next person agrees and takes it further, the next extends it again and the next adds something else, in a similar way to the example above.

- **People in the Venue**
  Think about commenting on other people in the same venue, but not too nearby. These comments can enrich a conversation, but take great care not to let anyone hear an uncomplimentary comment made about them. Discuss whether and how you would comment on:

  - a person's great height, at a pub with low beams
  - the bride's dress and appearance, at her wedding
  - the outfit of a guest at a fancy-dress party
  - the way someone, or a group of people, is/are behaving
  - a lady's unusual handbag, hat or scarf
  - the similarity between a person at your workplace/college and somebody famous
  - the similarity between children in a family photo
  - someone's tattoos
  - a person's job or the subject they study at college
  - a person's weight.

- **Talking Points**
  Discuss the type of comment you could make that would be directed towards your conversation partner. Try to find something unusual to comment about, so it could be, for example, earrings that look like little teacups or sharks, an antique-looking necklace, a tie with an amusing design on it, any accessories worn for a Christmas party (antlers, flashing brooches etc). T-shirt messages are often worn specifically to create a talking point so they are often worthwhile mentioning. The comment would often begin with: "I like your …" and add something appropriate and specific such as "How unusual" or "That's really funny". (For further advice on offering compliments please see the 'Compliments' chapter.)

- **Observations**
  Discuss the very subtle art of adding polite observations about your conversation partner, their possessions or their home, for example: "I do like the way you're always early" or "I like your house, it's so comfortable and warm" and so on. You need to smile as you make these types of comments and the content needs to be carefully chosen. Try making polite observations about each other in the group – of course you cannot do this early in the life of the group, you need to wait until everyone is familiar with each other.

- **Dressing Up**
  Agree that at the next group therapy session everyone will bring or wear a different accessory that they think might promote a comment from the others in the group. Each person then notices and comments on one other group member's interesting clothes, accessories or footwear.

- **Accessorize**
  Another connected activity is to collect images of accessories (some high street shops provide catalogues) and talk about the kinds of comments you could make about them.

Noticing, commenting and making polite observations 'credit cards' for homework

---

Today I'll study surroundings shown on TV, for example, the studio of a sports programme; the mascot of a pub in a TV 'soap'; the grounds of a stately home in a programme about antiques. I'll be critical for this task and report my thoughts back to the group.

Today I'm going to try to notice and comment on my surroundings at work. I'll be positive and report my thoughts back to the group.

Today I'm going to try to notice an unusual item worn by someone on TV and make a comment about it to someone else watching the same programme.

Today I'm going to try to notice any new or unusual item worn by a member of my family and make a nice comment about it.

Today I'm going to try to find the opportunity to notice and comment positively on two people at a social event.

Today I'm going to sit in a café with a close friend or family member and try to notice and comment on more than three people in the café. I'll take care to be quiet so that only my friend or family member can hear. I'll make the comments positive.

THE SOCIAL CV

Self-assessment questionnaire

On a scale of 1–10, where 1 is shy and 10 is confident, how do you feel about making use of your life experiences to add to the conversation with the following people:

- just one friend?
- a new friend of the opposite sex?
- a mixed group of friends?
- new people in a social setting?
- colleagues in a workplace setting?

People sometimes worry about whether they are up to the task of having conversations. They doubt whether they will seem sufficiently 'world-wise' to be able to speak from experience on a topic, 'well-versed' enough to be able to offer useful opinions or interesting enough to add a bit of colour to the flow of the chat. This chapter examines ways in which you might start to recognise your value in social settings. The things you find out about yourself, your history and your interests can all feed into your conversation at some point. When we find we have something 'in common' with our conversation partners we feel a kind of link, or bond, that can increase the warmth of the conversation or become the start of a friendship, or build on an existing one.

One point to be aware of, though, is not to feel you have to use your Social CV in every conversation, or at great length; a light touch is needed. Remember that for most people the most interesting thing in the world is themselves! So don't forget to ask them about their background and interests too, because that is how conversations work; along with balancing the mechanics of turn-taking we need to balance the information given by each person.

Try these exercises

- **Discuss**
  Please start by beginning to fill in the Social CV form at the end of this chapter. You will find, over time – don't try to do it all straight away – that there is a lot about you that you may be forgetting about. You are an interesting person and this will be reflected in your CV, which is a kind of brief autobiography. By filling this in you will acknowledge which sorts of things you are interested in and be able to talk about them with your conversation partner.

- **But Everyone Else has Trainers Like That!**
  Discuss in the group the values of uniqueness, versus those of 'fitting in'. Why do some teenagers want to wear exactly the same brand of clothing or shoes as their friend does? Why do others resent what they see as 'copying' when another person buys the same brand?

- **Three Sayings to Consider**
  Discuss the meaning behind the saying 'Keeping up with the Joneses'.

  Think of and discuss together in the group several scenarios that demonstrate what is meant by 'Imitation is the sincerest form of flattery'.

  Now discuss the saying 'You are unique just like everybody else'. Discuss whether it is possible to fit in and yet hold different values.

- **Poster**
  Make a 'Good Things About Me' poster. You will need a photo or drawing, or a symbol that stands for you. Stick this at the top of the page. Underneath, list all the good things about you. These can be anything from having a nice smile to having good clothes sense, to being good at chess or football, to knowing a lot about films, to having good academic qualifications, to character traits like being a good listener or good at enjoying people's jokes, or to being a good driver/cyclist. A similar diagram is a 'Mind Map' or spidergram, with yourself in the middle as described below. Please see Tony Buzan's work on 'Mind Maps'.

- **Spider's Nests**
  This builds on the previous exercise. Each person in the group makes a spidergram separately, preferably without being able to see each other's results. On a large sheet of paper (A3) put your name in an oval shape in the middle to form the 'body' of the spider and add eight fairly short legs. At the end of each leg write down a very general, core area of interest that you have; these could be leisure activities such as cinema, walking, art, DIY, cookery, collecting things, music, sports and so on, as well as friends, family and pets. Encircle each of these interests. There should be plenty of space left around the edge of your spider's 'feet' which now become new 'bodies'. Now extend the general, core interests by adding eight short legs to each of these new bodies, so for example if you had written 'cookery' as one of your core interests you now add eight subset interests to do with cookery – this could be cookery books, cookery programmes on TV, making curries, entertaining, making sweets, baking cakes, being a gourmet or visiting cafés, so these are subsets of the original eight core interests.

Eventually everyone in the group could have as many as 64 specific subsets of their interests attached to their original core eight.

Discuss in the group what the term 'in common' means.

Now compare spidergrams — find where the similarities are and where the differences lie. You will probably find that people have some areas in common and some areas of uniqueness. Sometimes the areas in common stem from completely different core interests, for example, a person with an interest in cookery might say they like making curries, while a person who enjoys watching football might enjoy visiting an Indian restaurant with their friends afterwards for a curry. Here their differing core interests come together because of the interest subsets. Finding things in common is helpful to a friendship/relationship.

Spidergram

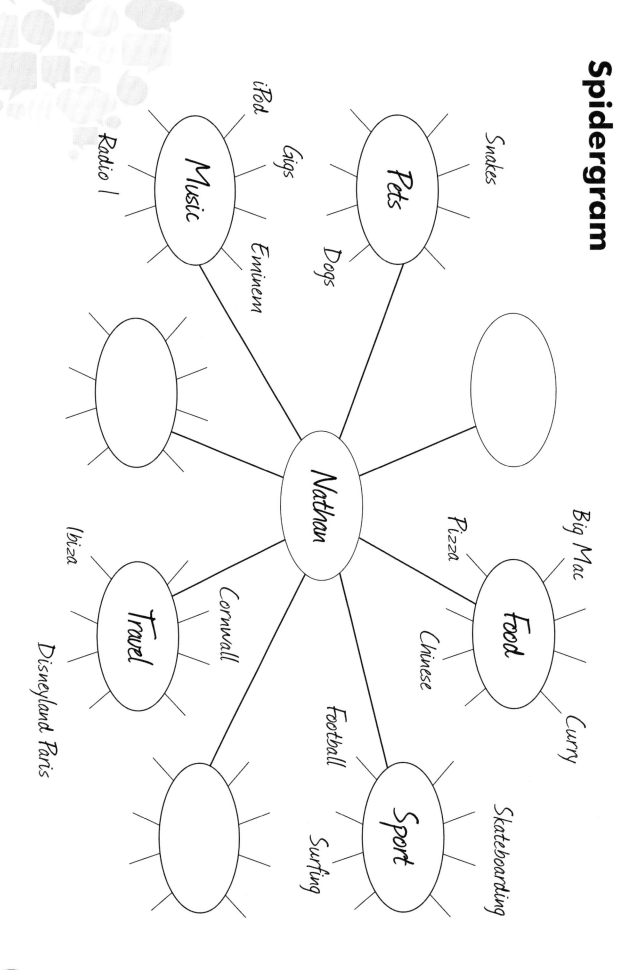

THE SOCIAL CV

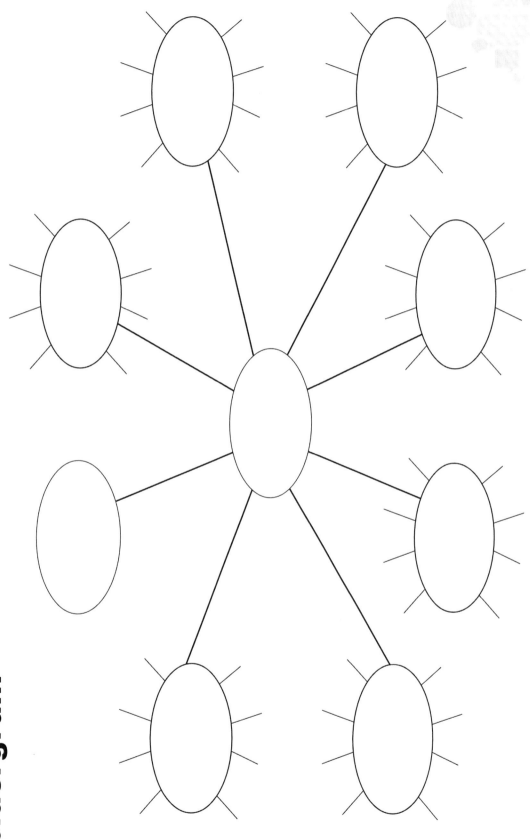

Spidergram

The Social CV 'credit cards' for homework

> Today I'm going to consider and write down any extra core interests that I could add to my Social CV.

> This week I'll listen to 'Desert Island Discs' and note any interesting things about the interviewee, including their background, what made them famous, their choices of records, luxuries and books. I'll report back to the group.

> Today I'm going to think of, and write down, any funny things that have happened to me.

> Today I'm going to research a TV celebrity and write down as many of their main core interests as I can discover, adding as many subset interests as I can. Do any of their interests overlap with mine?

> Today I'm going to try to include a mention of a core interest item on my Social CV in a conversation with people at home. If I can, I'll add a subset interest.

> Today I'm going to try to include a mention of a historical item on my Social CV in a conversation with someone at work/college. If I can, I'll add a subset interest.

THE SOCIAL CV

Please note that there are plenty of other homework possibilities to carry out for this chapter. These are connected with researching your history, your town and so on, as shown in the Social CV form. Because there is a lot to do, it is a good idea to treat this as ongoing work, which might last for months. Just tackle a bit at a time; if you try to do it all too quickly you run the risk of forgetting the information that you have found out. You might like to collate into a notebook all the information that you gather.

Please see overleaf for the 'My Social CV' ideas.

My Social CV

When I was born
What else happened in the world that year? (It could be the birth of a celebrity, the beginning or end of a war or conflict, an important political or economic crisis, the year connected with a particular invention etc). Research this item.

Where I was born
What else, apart from my birth, is interesting about that town/country? Maybe a well-known historic or current person was born there (this could be worth researching too – the Visitor's Centre or Tourist Information Centre will have information).

Places where I have lived
Again, these countries or towns can become talking points in a conversation, so try to find out anything of interest about people who lived there or things that the place is famous for.

Where I live now
This is also worth researching if you haven't already done so. Again, look in the local Visitor's Centre or Tourist Information Centre for information. Are there points of interest in the town? These could be good shops, leisure centres, museums, parks and 'attractions'. Consider visiting them. Walk around the town and look for the blue plaques on the walls of some houses – these show the names of any noteworthy people who lived there and why they were famous. If you actually visit the places you will find them easier to remember and therefore easier to mention in a conversation.

My childhood family/my background/who brought me up
This is highly personal; some people prefer not to delve into their family history. However, if you feel OK to research this you may find out interesting things about your family that are worth remembering, for example, your aunt might live in an interesting place or your grandfather might have had an interesting job or maybe he worked in an industry that no longer exists. Someone in your family might have been awarded a medal for sport or military service, or perhaps knew someone famous.

Linked to the above – my current family, my partner, my husband/wife
You don't need to 'announce' that you are already in a long-term relationship but it is good manners to make it known, just in case the conversation partner thinks that you are 'available'. You could mention that you and your partner both like the same things or how you differ. Sometimes it is appropriate to mention how you met your partner or perhaps where you went on honeymoon. Children very often become the subject of conversation but this topic can become irritating if it starts to become competitive in the areas of their academic or other achievements. Be humble!

Memories of my early childhood
Include things you enjoyed as a child, such as favourite foods, holidays, activities, days out, funny little quirks you had at that time and anything else. You might extend your knowledge of your childhood self by asking members of your family what they remember about you at that time.

Things I learned at school and at college
Any lessons on your curriculum that might have been unusual or different from another person's educational experience? Any crafts? By the way, for use in conversations it's best to try not to be competitive about your achievements as some people might view this as bragging and therefore a put-off.

Students I met who made an impression on me – and why
This could be someone who you remember as a particular kind of character: the class clown, the bully, the kind person, someone who had difficulties and how they coped.

Teachers I met who made an impression on me – and why
Again, there were probably a few who stood out as amusing characters, good at their job or you can even mention those who had negative characteristics.

My 'Desert Island Discs'
Think of your favourite music, books and luxuries you couldn't do without.

Holidays I have had
Think of where you went, how the journey was, what special events took place.

My favourite pastimes, hobbies
What do you do in the evenings and at weekends? If you like trips out, where do you go?

Sports I like to play
Don't forget activities like walking, darts or snooker, which you might not at first consider to be sports.

Sports I like to watch
Include live events at the stadium, pitch, track and so on, as well as those on TV.

My kind of film
Because this can be a common topic of conversation and can influence others' opinions about you, my advice is to try to extend your experience in this area if you can and especially if your preferences are narrow or restricted to horror films, romantic comedies or other genres. Other people might not like these, so might prefer not to go to a cinema with you. You can also extend your knowledge of films by watching film review shows on TV.

Interesting people I've met
Don't feel this needs to be restricted to famous people; we seldom meet them, but we do meet neighbours and friends who have had unusual and interesting lives or experiences.

My skills
Can you put up a shelf? Clean a house? Sort out a computer problem? Knit? Grow your own vegetables? Change a bicycle tyre? Make cakes? This is often a good topic of conversation as the conversation partner might also have an interest in this, or might have a difficulty with one of these tasks and need advice or help, or you might ask for advice and help from them. This can lead to a basis for friendship as long as the task requested is not arduous!

My job
This can be an interesting topic of conversation; however, people often define themselves by their job title, which tends to limit their self-image. Yes, do mention your job, but try to talk about aspects of the work – what it involves, the ups and downs of it, and the other types of people who work there. These might resonate with aspects of the conversation partner's job.

Don't feel ashamed of being unemployed, this is common these days and is probably not your fault anyway. If you prefer not to talk about this you could mention that you are looking for employment but that at the moment you have other things to do that take up your time. Then move on to another topic. If on the other hand the conversation partner is unemployed but you have a job it's wise to be sensitive about that and not to talk too much about your work; instead you could mention that it is good that they have time to pursue their interests.

My party tricks
Tread carefully with this one; remember that once you have mentioned that you sometimes put both your legs around the back of your neck or can play 'Happy Birthday' by tapping on your teeth, you will be asked to do it! However, as long as you are confident about it and feel happy to perform, you have a good conversation topic and will be remembered in a good light.

THE SOCIAL CV

Here is a blank Social CV form for you to complete.

My Social CV

1 When I was born

2 Where I was born

3 Places where I have lived

4 Where I live now

5 My childhood family/my background/who brought me up

6 Linked to the above – my current family, my partner, my husband/wife

7   Memories of my early childhood

8   Things I learned at school and at college

9   Students I met who made an impression on me – and why

10   Teachers I met who made an impression on me – and why

11   My 'Desert Island Discs'

THE SOCIAL CV

12 Holidays I have had

13 My favourite pastimes, hobbies

14 Sports I like to play

15 Sports I like to watch

16 My kind of film

17 Interesting people I've met

18 My skills

19 My job

20 My party tricks

USING HUMOUR

Self-assessment questionnaire

On a scale of 1–10, where 1 is difficult and 10 is easy, how do you feel about:

- *using humour with one friend?*
- *using humour with a group of friends?*
- *remembering and telling jokes?*
- *using humorous self-deprecation?*
- *using humorous anecdotes?*

Things that make us smile or laugh will cheer up the day. If you can manage to include an element of humour in your conversations you may be able to make someone else smile too. The easiest way to introduce humour is to ask whether your conversation partner has seen a recent funny TV programme or film. If they have you will be able to compare notes about the funniest bits. A tip – often the best scenes in a comedy film are the ones they use for the trailers.

Another way is to make use of funny things that have happened to you, that is, funny anecdotes. You will have to be prepared to laugh at yourself and be laughed at a bit, but people like speakers who use self-deprecation because it shows a level of humility. Some stand-up comics are masters of this kind of humour; watch them for the kinds of funny stories they tell about themselves and how they tell them.

You are aiming to lighten conversation by using humour rather than trying to be a comedian, but it is worthwhile learning, say, three jokes, the clean sort that you could tell an auntie. Some jokes may seem rather childish, but don't ignore them, at least to start with. As you increase your repertoire you will come across some jokes which are more suitable for your age. It can be difficult to remember jokes, so write down any that you find funny and re-read them from time to time to keep them in your mind.

The difficult part is in knowing when and how to shoehorn jokes into a conversation. Sometimes the opportunity is handed to you; the other speaker might mention, for example, her great difficulty in building a garden shed and you can make a pun about shedding tears over it. At other times, when perhaps there's a lull in the chat, you could simply say: "I heard this funny joke the other day, I must tell you", and then add your joke. Don't do this too often or it will sound contrived. Perhaps a reasonable humour rate is one or two jokes or puns per conversation. Try not to repeat the same joke to a person the next time you chat.

A word of warning – try not to confuse humour with rudeness; a good joke will amuse even quite prim people, but risqué jokes can offend. Rudeness doesn't only apply to sexual innuendo; it also refers to the need to avoid racist, ageist and other unfortunate types of humour. If in doubt don't tell the joke or try it out tentatively on one close and trusted friend first.

Try these exercises

- **Comedy Shows**

    Watch and listen to as many funny TV or radio programmes as you can and go to see funny films or remember some that you have already seen. You will probably find that there are different kinds of humour such as those in the following list. Try to think of specific examples of each of the following types. The first has been begun for you, but add to it if you can:

    - *physical, 'slapstick' humour, two types:*

        'Mr Bean' (which is intentional and rehearsed)

        'You've Been Framed!' (unintentional, often an accident) and many items on YouTube

    - *sitcoms*

    - *stand-up comedy*

    - *satire*

    - *romantic comedies*

    - *funny quizzes.*

    Now, as a group discuss which types of humour you like and try to think why. Which programmes or films use elements of humour in a realistic way that you could talk about or even copy? (But don't copy slapstick humour, it could hurt someone and therefore lose you friends.)

USING HUMOUR

- **Anecdotes**
  What are the funniest things that have ever happened to you or someone you know? Now think of some funny things that have happened recently. Share these true and funny anecdotes in the group sessions.

  Examples of anecdotes:

  I once nearly drove off in the wrong car – my son had given me the old and worn key to his old car and asked me to collect it from a car park. I found what I thought was his car (same make and colour), unlocked it, started the engine, noticed the alarm going off and then realised that I should have got into the car just beside this one. Luckily the real owner didn't find me doing this!!

  My brother-in-law once fell asleep during an interview for a job!

- **Laughter Club**
  Just practise laughing; watching someone else laugh will almost certainly make you feel like laughing too. Practise smiling at yourself in the mirror. In a group therapy setting try walking round the room, smiling, breathing in quite deeply and then on the out breath say a slow, "Ha Ha Ha". Add a shaking movement of the shoulders. Now speed this up until you are really laughing and enjoying the laughter of others.

- **Laughing Till You Cry**
  Have you ever watched someone laugh so much that they start to ooze tears? Or heard them say, "I laughed till I cried"? Discuss the effect this had on you. Also think of the effect of watching babies and very young children laugh helplessly (you can sometimes find good examples of this on TV or YouTube).

- **Going Crackers**
  Examine jokes – how they are made and how to make up some of your own. For this you will need lots of examples of jokes and a free resource will be there if you save jokes from Christmas crackers. Look out for the core component of the joke, which is very often a word that has two meanings. Please see 'Save your cracker jokes' in the Appendices. Also collect jokes from comedy shows on TV or radio.

The using humour 'credit cards' for homework

Today I'm going to look out for something funny that someone does at coffee or tea break at work.	Today I'm going to try to learn a 'Knock Knock' joke.
Today I'm going to learn a 'Doctor, Doctor' joke.	Today I'm going to try to jot down and learn a joke that I hear in a TV programme.
Today, within a conversation, I'm going to try telling my neighbour about something true but funny that happened to me.	Today, within a conversation, I'm going to try telling someone at work/college about something true but funny that happened to me.

COMPLIMENTS

Self-assessment questionnaire

On a scale of 1–10, where 1 is difficult and 10 is easy, how do you feel about compliments – (1) giving them and (2) receiving them – with the following people:

- *just one friend of the same sex as you?*
- *just one friend of the opposite sex?*
- *a mixed group of friends?*
- *new people at a casual occasion?*
- *workplace people in a formal setting such as a meeting?*

A good compliment given at the right moment can warm a conversation, further a friendship and even oil the wheels of negotiations, going way beyond the basic exchange of information between people. Complimenting can indicate that you are interested enough in a person to notice details about them, and therefore that you have been thinking about them and care. In the more formal setting of a negotiation at work or even in international politics, a compliment is an indication of respect towards the other 'side'.

This chapter looks at ways to give compliments and how to receive them.

Giving a compliment

Compliments tend to mean more to the receiver if they are specific rather than general. Suppose someone pays a compliment such as: "You look nice" or "That's a good piece of work", or "That was good." These are all welcome comments, but very general. Now suppose the compliments added reasons for their positivity: "You look nice, that colour really suits you" or "That's a good piece of work; you have mentioned all the issues we looked at during the meeting", or "That was good, I always love curry, but your version is great, just the right amount of spice." These extended and specific forms sound much more genuine.

Note that not all the examples of compliments given above are about visual things and that's important; a compliment doesn't have to be about appearance; often compliments about a person's work or achievements will be appreciated even more.

Receiving a compliment

Do you secretly cringe when someone offers you a compliment? Do you just say, "Yes" or "Yes, I know" when someone says your work is good? Do you say something like: "I've had it for years" if they say they like your jumper or "It's a bit dry/soggy/fattening" and so on if they compliment you on the cake you made?

Sometimes it can feel embarrassing when someone gives us a compliment, and in the speedy to and fro of conversation it is sometimes difficult to think quickly how to respond in the best way. To prevent this sort of embarrassment it's a good idea to have a few stock responses ready and to have rehearsed them several times.

These are the sorts of responses to go for:

"Thank you!" or "Thanks, much appreciated", both accompanied by a warm smile. This will be OK for many occasions.

An even better technique, is the 'ping-pong' trick, for example, if they compliment you on your new haircut 'bat it back' to them by saying, "Thanks for noticing" or "Thank you …" plus a comment like, "I had it done yesterday". Another ping-pong response would be, "Thank you" and then say something complimentary back to them, such as: "Your top is a lovely colour."

Try to avoid belittling the compliment just offered, so if they say: "That's a really nice jacket" try not to react with something like: "Oh, this thing? I've had it for ages!" because then they will feel that the compliment was misplaced or offered too late. Much better to say: "Thanks, yes, I'm fond of it" and then follow up with: "You look great too …" adding a compliment in return.

Try these exercises

- **Spot the Compliment**
  Spot and discuss any compliments that you can find within the following statements:

  - *You look great today, I like the way you have done your hair.*

  - *Thanks to your advice I chose the coach and not the train for my journey to London.*

  - *You have made a big chocolate cake.*

  - *You have made a wonderful chocolate cake.*

COMPLIMENTS

- *Your hat is the same colour as your scarf.*
- *What a good idea!*
- *Well done for getting here on time.*
- *Your house has a lot of cupboards.*
- *Shall I compare thee to a summer's day? Thou art more lovely and more temperate.*
- *Wow! Hasn't your flat got lovely views, you did well to rent it quickly before anyone else found it.*

- **Offer a Compliment**

  Together brainstorm the kinds of compliments that people give about the following things and the best types of responses to those compliments:

  - a meal/a cake cooked by a friend
  - a friend's sporting achievement
  - a person's academic achievement
  - a friend's house
  - someone's pet
  - a friend's car
  - a girl's clothes and hair
  - a man's clothes
  - a friend's girlfriend/boyfriend.

- **Valentines**

  Look at some examples of love poetry or lyrics of love songs. Find the compliments and discuss the effect on the person whom the writer might be addressing.

- **Circle of Compliments**

  For a group try a 'Circle of compliments', that is, saying something complimentary but specific, about the person to your left, who must give a 'ping-pong' response. They then turn to their left and compliment the next person who 'ping-pongs' back, and so on round the circle.

- **Cumulative Compliments**
This game is for a group. Each person has a piece of paper on which they write their name. They pass the paper on to the next person who writes something positive and complimentary about the person named, and passes it on to the next group member. Everyone will receive several compliments and thinks about good responses. Discuss with the group two of the comments and responses for each person, preferably one that they find it easy to respond to and one that is more difficult. How does it make you feel when you are complimented? How does it feel to give a compliment to someone else? How would someone feel if no one had a good thing to say about them?

Compliments 'credit cards' for homework

> Today I'll listen for three compliments given by a radio or TV interviewer. I'll note the programme details, what the compliment was, how it was given (Did it sound genuine? Was it specific?) and report back to the therapy session.

> Today I'm going to listen to a TV or radio drama, and make a note of as many general and specific compliments included in the drama as I can, and report them back to the therapy session.

> Today I'm going to pay a genuine and specific compliment to someone at home. If someone compliments me I'll thank them, and if it's appropriate I'll say, "Thanks for noticing". I'll report back to the therapy session.

> Today I'm going to pay a genuine compliment to someone at work. If someone compliments me I'll thank them, and if it's appropriate I'll say, "Thanks for noticing". I'll report back to the therapy session.

> Today I'll compliment someone at a social event (for example, a party, evening class, meeting with friends at a pub). If someone compliments me I'll thank them and if appropriate I'll say, "Thanks for noticing". I'll report back to the therapy session.

> Today I'll compliment someone during a phone call. If the person compliments me I'll thank them, and if appropriate I'll say, "Thanks for noticing". I'll report back to the therapy session.

CRITICISM AND COMPLAINTS   19

Self-assessment questionnaire

On a scale of 1–10, where 1 is difficult and 10 is easy, how do you feel about criticism and complaints – (1) giving them and (2) receiving them – with the following people:

- *a member of your family?*
- *a friend?*
- *staff at a small café?*
- *management staff at the place where you work?*
- *the management of a large chain store?*
- *the management of a large organisation such as a school or hospital?*

It would be great if we never had to criticise anyone or make a complaint, but sometimes situations arise in which we need to point out a mistake. If we can do this without making a person feel resentful then it's likely that a good relationship can be maintained or even improved.

Sometimes we are criticised ourselves and it's important to know how to accept a criticism politely but in a way that maintains our self-respect and a good relationship with the critic.

This chapter focuses on criticisms that come about in everyday conversation and also mentions more formal complaints.

The 'praise sandwich'

This is the most useful tool in the critic's box. It means starting with some praise, following with the criticism, then finishing with another statement of praise or positivity. For example, suppose a child makes you a cup of tea but omits to use boiling water. Using the praise sandwich technique you could say: "How lovely, what a kind idea. It's best to boil the water, but not to worry, it's so nicely presented on that tray." This way you have been positive, full of praise and at the same time educated them in the art of tea making. You will, of course, have to drink the tea they've made, so that the small criticism doesn't hurt their feelings!

Suppose your flatmate or partner has done your washing for you but shrunk your jumper. You could say: "You are so kind to do my washing. I use a cooler wash for delicates so that they don't shrink like this one, but everything else is fine, thanks so much."

At work a colleague has started a massive amount of photocopying at a time when you had said you needed to copy an important document. You could try: "Wow, you are way ahead. I was hoping to finish this today. You are really quick and efficient."

Your friend asks you how they look. There is a problem. Try: "Your hair looks great and that green top is beautiful. The skirt seems a bit loose, but everything else looks lovely."

The sandwich system can be used in a very light way during a chat with a friend. Suppose you are talking about a film you both saw, which she liked but you did not really enjoy. Your friend says: "I loved all the singing and dancing, and the costumes." Your sandwich response could be: "Yes, it was really colourful. I thought it was a little bit too long, but what good visual impact."

A polite complaint

Sometimes we need to return faulty goods, complain about the quality of food in a restaurant or make a formal complaint about conditions at work.

In all these cases it's important to remain polite and to be clear about what you expect to be done in order to put things right. It's helpful to know your consumer rights, but not to make too much of an issue about that as it can appear to be confrontational. You are aiming to strike a balance where you are not too meek and passive, but not too aggressive either. Somewhere in the middle is assertive, where you state your case clearly but politely.

If you have bought a garment which turns out to have a hole in it when you get home, the key things are to take it back as soon as you can, explain the problem and ask for a replacement. However, if the problem is that when you get home and try it on again you realise that you don't really like it then it's wise to keep the receipt and present it when you return the item.

Sale goods are not always returnable.

If your food is bad at a café you need to make the complaint before you have eaten very much of it, otherwise it just looks as if you are trying to get extra for free. It's best to be specific and say that, for example, you find the potatoes are undercooked. Explain that you would like a different dish rather than risk the same again. Sometimes the manager will reduce the cost of the meal, or offer a free pudding or glass of wine. If you have been ill after a meal out then it's important to make a complaint so that they will put things right and avoid making others ill! Be polite but straightforward when you complain, don't add moans and grumbles, and the chances are that they will offer a refund or a free meal at another time.

CRITICISM AND COMPLAINTS

Accepting criticism

If you are criticised does this make you feel really bad? It's important to separate the helpful critical comments from a real complaint, a general grumble aimed at you, or an unfair criticism.

If a teacher says that your music composition would be better if you included more vocals then don't be offended or take this as hurtful criticism, try to see it as helpful advice from a more experienced person. (They should have used the 'praise sandwich'!)

If you are late for a date it's best to apologise and add something to show that your apology is genuine, for example, you could say: "I'm so sorry to have kept you waiting, it must have been a real nuisance for you to stand here for 10 minutes in the rain."

If you are unfairly criticised, for example: "You always leave the lights on" when you know that you don't, then you will need to point out that this is not the case. You could add an offer that you would be happy to check that lights are out if they would like you to.

Try these exercises

- **Discuss and Role Play**

    Discuss and role play the following. You will need one complainer and one member of staff:

    - ask for a replacement prawn cocktail starter because your dish tastes odd

    - take back a CD that has a scratch on it

    - phone a local radio station to say that they forgot to include your school on the 'Closed due to snow' list

    - return a jacket you bought two weeks ago. The seam was poorly stitched so that it is already coming apart. You have not kept the receipt

    - word a formal, written complaint to a supermarket complaining that you had to wait 10 minutes to be served because only one till was being used

- **Legitimate Grumbles?**

    Is it reasonable to complain about the following:

    - the coconut cake you bought, not realising it contained coconut?

    - a late train which made you miss your connection?

    - a faulty cable on a new lamp?

- *the instructions accompanying a piece of self-assembly furniture?*
- *someone's cat that misbehaved in your garden?*
- *a friend's dog that bit your child?*
- *the cost of a cinema ticket?*

- **The Gas Man Cometh**
  Find the lyrics of the humorous Flanders and Swann song 'The Gas Man Cometh' (it is on YouTube), and together discuss whether and how you would complain about all the poor quality workmanship.

- **Praise Sandwiches**
  For a group try a 'Round of praise sandwiches'. Prepare by asking each member of the group to slightly spoil the way they look – could be messing up their hair, smudging their lipstick, putting their jumper on inside out, making a biro smear on their face (take care that it is not indelible ink though!), tucking part of their jacket into their trousers and so on. Now take it in turns to offer a praise sandwich to someone else, for example: "What a nice jacket. You've got it slightly tucked into your trousers by the way. I love the shoes."

- **Criticise Me**
  Try a criticism practice. Each member of the group is accused of always being late and must answer in an assertive way.

CRITICISM AND COMPLAINTS

Criticism and complaints 'credit cards' for homework

> Today I'll listen for any criticisms made by a radio or TV interviewer against a politician. I'll note the programme details, what the criticism was and how it was given. I'll report my findings back to the therapy session.

> Today I'm going to listen to a TV or radio drama, and make a note of as many complaints and criticisms included in the drama as I can, and report them back to the therapy session.

> Today, if there is an opportunity and it's appropriate, I'll make a complaint to a shop where something I have bought is faulty.

> In the time before the next group session I'll make a list of things I could have complained about in the past but didn't.

> Today I'll try to find an opportunity to offer a 'praise sandwich' to someone in my family.

> Today I'll try to find an opportunity to offer a 'praise sandwich' to someone at work.

REMINISCING AND REFLECTING

Self-assessment questionnaire

On a scale of 1–10, where 1 is difficult and 10 is easy, how do you feel about reminiscing and reflecting with:

- *parents?*
- *siblings?*
- *grandparents and elderly people in general?*
- *old school friends?*
- *newer friends with a shorter history?*

A very useful skill to extend your conversation topic choices, add humour or poignancy and often to create a closer bond is to be able to find common memories to discuss and preferably smile about.

Linked to this is the ability to draw out of people some memories that you can't share (perhaps the memories are from a time before you were born), but which could still be talked about from your perspective as well as theirs.

With family and old friends reminiscence topics will often start with: "Do you remember when we used to …" Note that their recollection will not be exactly the same as yours. A mother may remember summer holidays of years ago as times of arranging for her child's happiness and well-being but at the cost of her own energy and patience, while the child may just remember happy days of playing or being taken out. Take very great care not to contradict people who remember things differently from you, their memory is their memory; you are not trying to find a forensically provable truth, but to increase the pleasant quality of conversation. One person may begin with: "Do you remember that every Friday on our way to Brownies we used to pop in to the shop and buy sweets?" whereas you remember that Brownies was on Wednesday and that it was cake that you used to buy. Don't argue about that; what does it matter?

If you try reminiscence conversations with elderly people you will usually find that they are pleased, even flattered to recount experiences of their lives and that they will regard you as extremely polite if you show you are listening. The benefits for you are that their stories could be very interesting; you may learn facts about the past and you should be able to extend the conversation this way. It's best to allow the conversation partner to select their memories, because there will be some that they might prefer not to dwell upon; the trick here is to use open rather than closed questions. Please see the chapter on 'Open and closed questions and invitations to speak' for further information on this. The kinds of open questions to try could begin with: "When you were my age lots of things must have been different; what sorts of things did you do when you weren't at school/work?" or "Could you tell me about fashion when you were a teenager? What did young people like to wear then?" or "I heard that life was quite hard in the forties, fifties etc when people had to make do with less, but I wondered whether there were also some good things too, what do you think?"

Try these exercises

- **Photos from the Album**
  Each member of the group brings to the SLT session some photos from their childhood or young adult life and/or some postcards they were sent years ago. Now pair up and ask each other four questions about the photos. The questions should focus on subjects such as:

  - where they lived at that time

  - what they were doing at school/college/work

  - who their friends were

  - any personal or world events that affected them at the time.

  The questioned person should try two brief, succinct answers and two longer, reflective ones. Which type of answer will become useful as a conversation extender, which will be interesting and when does the whole thing become boring?

  Alternatively, the old postcards can stimulate memories of the friends or members of their family who sent them and if a group member has collected some that they are willing to show then it would be useful to discuss, briefly, their recollections of the sender.

- **Reminiscence Questions**
  Make a list of the elderly people in your family or those you know otherwise, such as neighbours in your road. Bearing in mind their age try to think of some reminiscence topics for potential discussion with each one. These will be memories of times or events that you probably didn't experience yourself, but would please them to remember and share with you. Form your ideas into a series of open questions that you could ask.

Now try the same procedure for younger people; make a list of friends who you see often, of roughly your own age who have shared some of the same experiences as you and think how you could have a reminiscence conversation with them. Do this carefully and add as many mutual memories as you can think of because this list will be the most useful one in 'real life' outside the therapy setting.

Now try it again thinking of a list of friends from the past who you might sometime contact again.

Discuss your thoughts with the group or with the therapist and allow them to comment on your lists.

The following two exercises show how people's memories of the same thing can differ:

- **Where Was I at the Time?**
  Each member of the group tries to remember where they were or what they were doing at or around the time when a significant world event took place. These tend to be great tragedies or some royal occasions, for example: an assassination, the death of Diana, Princess of Wales, the start of a war, the election of a Prime Minister or a President, a royal wedding, an earthquake or tsunami of great proportions. Discuss the group's differing memories of the event itself and of what they were doing at that time.

- **Photofit**
  This is another memory game, based on remembering faces, not directly reminiscing, but it is a useful exercise to practise prompting people to recall the people you want to discuss. You need to buy this (inexpensive) children's detective game, available from stationers and party shops. In the therapy group decide on a person you all know and individually try to create the features and details using the blank body and facial features provided in the box. Compare your results.

Now individually choose and describe in words only a person all other members of the group will know. See how long it takes for everyone to work out who it is. Now another group member thinks of and describes a different person, also known by all participants. It's often best to choose a celebrity as the subject for this game.

Is a verbal description or a photofit image a better way to describe someone?

Reminiscing and reflecting 'credit cards' for homework

Today I'm going to try to pick out a part of a TV conversation that is based on reflections and reminiscences of the characters. I'll make a note of it and report back to the group.	Today I'm going to try talking to a good friend about something we used to do when we were much younger.
Today I'm going to listen to a real conversation that other people are having, and try to pick out any parts which are based on reflections and reminiscences.	Today at coffee or tea break at school/college/university/work, I'm going to try to talk to a friend about something that happened on my first day there.
Today I'm going to try talking to a member of my family about something we used to do when we were much younger.	Today I'm going to try a reminiscence conversation with my neighbour or elderly relative. I'll focus on their memories rather than my own.

BEING OPTIMISTIC

Self-assessment questionnaire

On a scale of 1–10, where 1 is pessimistic and 10 is optimistic, how do you feel about being optimistic with the following people:

- *just one friend?*
- *a group of friends?*
- *relatives at a family gathering?*
- *a new acquaintance?*
- *a person in authority?*
- *an organisation?*

Consider for a moment the old expression 'Every cloud has a silver lining'. One explanation of the origin of this saying is that farmers used to worry about flooding, but the positive side for them would be that once the water had subsided, some good, damp soil, enriched by silt from upstream, would mean better crop production. The person who often says these words is the type who is optimistic and often a cheerful, heart-warming conversation partner who you would like to talk to again.

By contrast consider the 'Marvin Syndrome' (Marvin is a character from *The Hitchhiker's Guide to the Galaxy*, by Douglas Adams). This character is remorselessly gloomy and despite being helpful sometimes, would be quite depressing to talk to at length in real life. For example, in one episode he says: "Here I am, brain the size of a planet, and they tell me to take you up to the bridge. Call that job satisfaction? 'cause I don't." Another Marvin example: "I've asked for (my diodes) to be replaced, but no-one ever listens." His moans and groans are directed towards an organisation and suggest that, whatever he does, nothing will improve. In the book this is very funny, but in the real world when people direct moans vaguely to their workplace they don't actually deal with the problem. Usually a well-worded and politely delivered suggestion to a manager will end with a positive outcome eventually.

For further clarification about pessimism and its associated body language, picture (or look up on the internet) some of EH Shepard's images of Eeyore, the gloomy donkey from the 'Winnie the Pooh' stories. Although these are children's books and the character is not human, the images of Eeyore illustrate very well the drooping posture of the eternally negative. Consider the ways in which the body language of optimistic versus pessimistic people differs.

It is not recommended to be artificially cheery all the time or to point out the positive side of others' misfortunes, but to be positive about your own life is a real help in a conversation. It's best not to define yourself by your problems or to dwell on the down side of your life when chatting to others; everyone has problems and they may be depressed if you go on about yours too much. However, with an old friend or family member it is fine to explain why you may be looking a bit low and their support can help.

As a background to the reasons for feeling cheerful about yourself it's a good idea to read the chapter 'The Social CV' and to fill in the form at the end of that chapter.

Try these exercises

- **The 'Can Do' Attitude**

  Have you ever asked someone to do something for you only to be confronted by all sorts of negatives and reasons why they wouldn't do that, or say they can't or think it should be done a different way? Can you think of times when, on the other hand, you have been met with positivity and a 'can do' attitude? Discuss some occasions when these different attitudes have been presented to you and how you felt about that person or organisation.

  Now think of times when you have been asked to help with something (which actually you could do), but you could only think of reasons why not to do it and only a big "No" has come to your mind. How might other people regard you?

- **The Good News and the Bad News**

  This is an old party game in which one person states a piece of bad news, for example: "The bad news is that they say our summers are going to be cold and wet from now on." The next person counters this positively, for example, by saying that: "The good news is that it's a sunny day today." The next person begins their statement with: "But the bad news is that …" and adds a point such as "we might get sunburn." The next person adds: "But the good news is that …" and might suggest: "I have some excellent sun cream and a long-sleeved T-shirt" and so on round the circle. Take care to end the round on a positive note. It's best to have an odd number of people for this game otherwise the bad news will always be given by the same people.

- **Sayings**
  Discuss the meanings of the following sayings and add any more that the group can think of in a similar vein:

  - Always look on the bright side of life.
  - A smile doesn't cost anything.
  - Laugh and the world laughs with you, weep and you weep alone.
  - A little smile goes a long way.
  - A glass half-empty versus a glass half-full.

- **Have a Nice Day!**
  You may have noticed, particularly in American TV programmes or films, a habit of shop assistants, take-away café staff and so on, to end the transaction with the phrase above. It is often said in a way that seems insincere or superficial because it could have been something that the managers have instructed the staff to do. Discuss in the group how the phrase makes you feel and whether there is an alternative way of conveying positivity as you talk to people or in your business dealings.

- **Yes and ...**
  Discuss the feelings behind "Yes and ..." as opposed to "Yes, but ..." How often could you substitute a "Yes and ..." statement in your talk? Try making potentially disagreeable statements to each other in the group, such as: "Chicken sandwiches are the best", to which another person, let's say a vegetarian, will answer: "Yes, and cheese ones are great."

- **A Problem Shared is a Problem Halved**
  First of all discuss the meaning of this saying as a group. The point of the exercise is to show that discussing a problem can help to make our problems more bearable and allow us still to present ourselves in a cheerful way.

  Everyone in the group makes their own individual list down one side of a piece of paper of all the things that annoy or upset them. (Please see the homework task connected with this exercise as it's better to prepare for this before the session if possible.)

  Some of these annoyances will be trivial, such as the unexpected need for a coin to release one shopping trolley from the others and then finding that this one cannot be steered; the near impossibility of getting the wrapper off a new DVD; the rejection of your old clothes by a charity shop; or the habit of lettuce freezing onto the back of the fridge. These sorts of problems are probably shared by the whole group. They need to be laughed about. If you've never seen an episode of 'Grumpy Old Men' or 'Grumpy Old Women' it's worth watching to see how having a good grumble can be quite funny (especially in retrospect!).

After discussing each other's lists write beside your list of grumbles (a) how many others have had the same sorts of irritations in their lives or agree with your grumble and (b) add a large "Haha!" It's worth noting that some of the annoyances that we deem in retrospect to be funny can be used as humorous anecdotes to add to a conversation.

Some annoyances are slightly more frustrating, such as the length of the queue in the Post Office; the inevitability of your train being late on an important day when it has always been slightly early; the spill of curry sauce on your newly dry-cleaned pale jacket; the lack of a good signal when you are trying to make a call on your mobile phone. These frustrations can be sorted out and can even still be funny; watch TV shows with stand-up comedians for confirmation of this type of scenario.

Again, make a list of such frustrations you have experienced and then, after discussing each other's lists, write beside your listed items (a) how many others have experienced similar frustrations (b) how others sorted the problems out and (c) add a "Haha!" if in retrospect it can be seen as funny.

Some problems may be more complex, but still light enough for the group to be able to give support and encouragement, and it's very likely that other group members will have had similar problems. These could be problems at work, perhaps a manager who is always critical or a colleague who doesn't do their fair share.

Discussion could lead to action elsewhere, for example, a well-prepared meeting or at least a decision to log the occurrences of the problem. Perhaps the problems are to do with the behaviour of someone in the family. The group may discuss the idea of the 'win-win' attitude where if you correctly predict that, for example, the teenager will, as usual, slam the door, then congratulate yourself (silently) for predicting correctly rather than grumbling. If on the other hand he doesn't do it then you can celebrate! The 'win-win' strategy can also apply to your teacher who perhaps has a habit of repeating a particular phrase, a partner who forgets to turn off the lights and so on. Again, beside the listed problem write down the group's suggestions and solutions.

BEING OPTIMISTIC

Please note: Some problems are much more difficult to solve and may not be sorted out in the SLT setting at all. These may include health issues, relationship problems or money troubles. Group members may not want to discuss these difficulties in this setting, but sometimes it's worth just discussing the idea that if people have very serious problems there can still be positive outcomes of some kind, if the right professional help is sought.

Being optimistic 'credit cards' for homework

Today I'm going to listen to or watch a drama or 'soap' and make a note of people being optimistic, also those who are pessimistic in their interactions with others. I'll report back to the group.

Today I'm going to make a list of all the things that annoy me, starting with petty things and working towards more complex problems. I'll bring the list to the next session.

Today I'm going to observe people in a café/works canteen/school or college cafeteria buying their meal and see whether the waitress or server is cheery or gloomy in their manner.

Today I'm going to listen out for 'can do' comments made to me. I'll report back to the group.

Today I'm going to make three optimistic comments to people at home.

Today I'm going to try smiling and being optimistic even when something has just gone wrong for me or when I remember a problem.

BEING POSITIVE ABOUT OTHER PEOPLE

22

Self-assessment questionnaire

On a scale of 1–10, where 1 is awkward and 10 is perfectly comfortable, how do you feel about remaining positive about someone despite the disparaging remarks of:

- just one friend?
- a group of friends?
- a member of your family?
- all of your family?

It's very tempting to follow the newspaper columnists' example and make unkind/rude remarks about a person when they are not there, on the basis that being 'wickedly funny' is better than 'no fun at all'.

It can seem very humorous and in a way 'bonds' you with your conversation partner to comment in this way. Let's say the rude comment is about somebody's weight, clothes choice or behaviour for example. By commenting negatively about such matters you can feel that you are somehow in a 'not fat'/'not unfashionable'/'sensible by contrast' club together.

However, my advice is to avoid making this kind of remark. If you are rude about people behind their backs, your conversation partner will wonder what you say about them when they are not there. They might also feel free to make rude remarks about you to other people.

This strategy to avoid making negative remarks is particularly important when talking about people you know well. You are on safer ground when making wickedly funny remarks about politicians, celebrities and so on, who you are unlikely to meet. However, you still need to be a bit careful, because that politician, who becomes the butt of your jokes about being flabby, drunk, bald and so on, might be the one your conversation partner is going to vote for at the next election!

But what happens if your conversation partner is the one to make rude remarks? Joining in with the negative remarks, even if you do it superficially, can subtly undermine your own beliefs. Soon you could start really believing the rude remarks.

The situation will become even more complicated when there are three people involved in the conversation. By 'siding' with one you may alienate yourself from the other. It's much better to be true to your own thoughts.

Have you ever started the day thinking that the weather is OK, only to be confronted by someone who says: "It's a bit chilly isn't it?" It can be a challenge to stick with your original thoughts. In the same way it can be a challenge to resist taking on people's negative comments about others. The real trick is this: don't be tempted to join in, but try not to come across as disapproving either.

Try these exercises

- **Paparazzi**
  Look at photos and short articles about six well-known people. Choose articles that are rude or unkind about celebrities. (Cheap glossy magazines are a good source for such articles or columns in the broadsheets written by authors with known tendencies towards sarcasm.) Consider and discuss:

  - whether the comments are necessarily true

  - what the benefit for the journalist is in reporting (or making up) this item about this celebrity

  - whether we are being made to feel better about ourselves if we think we know that someone else, someone well-known, is worse than us at something.

- **Charm Offensive**
  Think of the kinds of rude comments people have made/might make about six people you know and then think of a comment that would satisfy your conversation partner without actually agreeing with them, for example: "He's so fat I wouldn't trust him to look after my biscuit tin," can be politely countered by: "Well, he's quite a warm and cuddly type of person, isn't he?" To "Her taste in fashion is really cheap-looking," the response could be: "She certainly likes to wear bright colours."

  Sometimes you might need to defend more robustly the absent acquaintance who is the target of the unkind remarks. It's still possible to remain polite while you say something like: "Well, I see where you are coming from but I've always found him to be ..." or "I think you have seen one side of his character, but ..."

  There are occasions when people spread rumours and lies or make racist or other prejudiced remarks. Be firm but polite in your response, taking care not to react too negatively because if you do the tendency may be for the comment-maker to feel pushed into being even more extreme.

Practise countering all three types of disparaging remarks in a 'Positive comments circle game'. You will need photos of people unknown to the group. These can be gathered from newspapers and magazines. One member of the circle shows a picture and makes a negative remark – it can be about something visible such as their clothes, or a hint about something to do with their character or behaviour. The next person in the group counters the remark but must remain polite. Then it's their turn to show a picture and make a negative comment which is dealt with by the next person and so on round the group.

- **The Good News and the Bad News**
  Please see the same heading in the previous chapter, 'Being optimistic', for details of how to play. Once you are familiar with this game you can use the same system to debate about a politician or celebrity: "The bad news is that this person (name a TV singing show contestant) sings out of tune," countered by: "But he has improved so much, I think he will be great after a few more lessons," then: "But he also looks wrong in that hat," countered by: "Well, it does make him stand out though," and so on.

  This can become a very sophisticated game if you use it to debate party manifestos at election times.

Being positive about other people 'credit cards' for homework

Today I'll read about a celebrity's behaviour in an incident as reported in a popular magazine and try to find a newspaper comment about the same incident. How are the articles different? I'll bring them to the next session to discuss.

I'll listen to a conversation in a 'soap' and note one character's negative comments made about a third person. I'll consider whether the conversation partner sticks to his own opinions about the victim of the comments or whether he is swayed and joins in with them. I'll discuss my findings at the next session.

Today I'll read about a celebrity's clothing/hairstyle etc as reported in a popular magazine. Are the comments valid or just cruel? Does the celebrity's appearance really matter? I'll bring the article and photo to the next session to discuss.

Today I'll eavesdrop on a conversation on public transport or in a queue. I'll listen for disparaging comments they make about another person. Is their conversation improved by this (is it funnier?) or do they just sound unkind? Or both?

Today I'll listen to humorous and satirical programmes on TV or radio. I'll focus my attention on negative comments made about politicians and make a note of them. I'll bring them to the next session for discussion.

Today I'm going to try to have a conversation with someone in which I'll make a positive comment about a mutual friend, or praise someone's good work or other quality. How does this affect the conversation?

ARGUMENT, MAKING A POINT AND DETACHMENT FROM YOUR OPINIONS

23

Self-assessment questionnaire

On a scale of 1–10, where 1 is very uncomfortable and 10 is perfectly comfortable, how do you feel about coping with disagreements and arguments with:

- *just one friend?*
- *a group of friends?*
- *relatives at a family gathering?*
- *a person in authority?*
- *an organisation?*

We tend to develop our ideas as we exchange them with those of other people. It is interesting and stimulating to talk to people with different thoughts from our own. Don't be offended if your conversation partner thinks differently from you; you can both benefit from a lively exchange of ideas.

However, we need to take a bit of care to avoid the situation where differences of opinion become arguments. You can never unsay things you've said, however much you apologise and regret. It is possible not only to spoil a conversation, but even to compromise a relationship by having an argument that does not end happily for all the speakers involved.

One difficulty about conversation is that most of us hold opinions about important topics such as religion, politics and the environment and can therefore contribute to debates, but these may not be the type of social exchange that is suitable for a friendly gathering. Instead we sometimes need 'small talk' for our conversations, rather than big ideas, grand statements and strongly expressed beliefs.

Differing recollections

Differences between recollections of events are not usually worth the argument – what does it matter which day of the week it was when you went to the shops? Is it important which route you took to get to your aunt's house? The trouble with expressing different recollections is that a simple chat can easily escalate into an argument, especially if someone then begins a sentence with: "You always …" or "I wish you wouldn't …" These sorts of statements can focus the whole conversation on people's behaviour within a relationship, when really the starting point was only a minor difference of recollection.

Consider this situation: a friend chats to you about an event at which you were both present, but as they recount the story you are aware that you recall things slightly differently. They are not actually lying, but just remember it differently. Is it worth contradicting them?

What if the person listening to the account is a police officer – would that change the need to contradict?

Differing preferences and entrenched opinions

It's great that people have different preferences; what if we all liked the same chocolate in a box? It's interesting and enriching to discover other people's favourite TV programmes, holiday destinations, leisure activities, books and so on that are different from our own. Sometimes, though, these preferences harden into entrenched opinions that disparage others' ideas. For example, one person may be a loyal Arsenal supporter while another is a keen Liverpool fan. That's fine, it's not worthwhile arguing about it. It's great that there are supporters for all the teams otherwise how could the leagues survive? Also, the top team varies a lot over time so avoid being triumphalist or defeatist – things are bound to change!

Similarly, entrenched opinions and dyed-in-the-wool prejudices can apply to political allegiances and cultural traditions. Sometimes you will profoundly disagree and may feel the need to stick to your opinions or principles. A key strategy here is to make sure you express your difference of the opinion itself rather than criticising the person holding that opinion. This way you can hold to your beliefs while at the same time coming across to your conversation partner as agreeable, easy-going and polite.

Differing opinions

If you feel that there is a controversial current event that you want to discuss, think carefully before you start. That topic might be difficult for others to discuss; it could bring out entrenched opinions and prejudices. It might be better to wait for someone else to introduce the topic or you could mention the subject as a question: "What did you think about … on the news last night?" then wait for others' thoughts before offering your own. It's usually best not to give the whole of your opinion about something right at the start – better to withhold some details so that you have room for manoeuvre.

ARGUMENT, MAKING A POINT AND DETACHMENT FROM YOUR OPINIONS

Spiders are related to crabs. No they're not! Yes they are! No they're not!

It is helpful to have some reference books available or access to the internet. Why argue over something that you can simply look up? When you first express your 'fact' about something it's best to do it tentatively: "I think it's true that spiders are somehow related to crabs." If someone expresses their 'fact' in a strident way to you, and you believe them to be incorrect, a good response is to just murmur "Interesting". You can always look up the facts later, just for your own information, if you don't want to be confrontational.

Try these exercises

- **Raking over the Coals**
  Consider times when you have observed or been involved in an argument, and how you felt about these exchanges. Jot down your reflections. Think in terms of:

  - arguments, even leading to violence, in plays, TV dramas or 'soaps'
  - negotiations between politicians or international heads of state
  - parent/teenage child rows over homework/staying out late/suitability of friends/helping out at home and so on
  - family rows at Christmas.

  Compare your experiences as a group. Discuss the triggers, whether the rows could have been avoided and how the various people involved could have extricated themselves from the quarrel.

- **Detachment Cubes**
  Rehearse 'detaching' yourself from an opinion which you hold, but which you don't want to be too forceful about when your conversation partner, who you like very much, holds the opposite opinion. Here are some 'detaching' ideas:

Best avoided	Better to substitute
"No"	"Maybe, but also"
"No, that's wrong"	"That's interesting, but I feel"
"You are stupid"	"That idea isn't so good"
"It was nothing like that"	"I remember it differently"
"You are lying"	"Was it like that? I thought …"
"They are stupid to do that"	"I suppose people think …"

Make or buy two large dice and write on each one six 'detaching' phrases such as those in the second column above, or think of others or use these:

"Mmm, although …", "On the other hand …", "Yes, though sometimes…", "And another way of looking at it would be …", "Or maybe …", "I can see where you're coming from on that, though …", "Yes, but it's just that …"

Now find some strong opinions that are not yours; they could come from newspapers ('Letters to the Editor' are often good examples of views that are strongly worded).

One person makes a strong statement. The next rolls the dice and begins a polite disagreement that starts with the phrase on the cube; again the opinion given need not really be their own, this is just an exercise. Now the next person takes a turn to make a strong statement and the next rolls the dice, and so on. Everyone needs to have the experience of expressing polite disagreement twice. Once the group feels comfortable and confident in expressing 'pretend' opinions you could try the same approach with some opinions that are really held.

- **Points of View**
  (You need to be part of a group for this game.) Arrange about 20 items on the table in a tight group, preferably with some tall items in the middle that hide smaller items from some participants' view. Sit around this arrangement and roughly sketch what you can see. Compare drawings and discuss the fact that the same grouping of items will look different depending on your direction of view. Just because one person's sketch looks different from another's, it doesn't make one right and the other wrong, they are equally correct. Try drawing the grouping of items as if you were the person on the other side of the table. Now you can begin to see things from their point of view.

  An extension to the previous idea is to look at a map of an area where there are several villages grouped around a hill and discuss the way the populations of those villages will see different faces of the hill, although it is still the same geographical feature.

  In just the same way people have different 'points of view', or opinions, about a news item, local event or political point.

- **Standing in Your Shoes**
  In pairs, draw around each other's shoes. One of the partners asks the other one questions about all sorts of subjects and adds background reasons for the

preferences or opinions. He then writes their name and opinions in the shoe outlines. For example: "I prefer to borrow movies on DVDs rather than go to the cinema because I don't like such a loud noise", "I am a vegetarian because I once saw a TV programme about abattoirs" or "I'm against pedestrian zones because they are scary at night." Try to fit in as many comments as possible. Now swap over and let the other partner do the interviewing and writing.

Conclude by having a discussion about the expression 'Standing in your shoes' and how it is possible to tolerate other people's ideas once you know why they feel as they do.

- **Sayings**
  Discuss the meanings of these sayings:

  "A moot point", "Raking over the coals", "The air was blue", "Opening up old wounds", "Going at it hammer and tongs", "A heated debate", "I have a bone to pick with you", "Six of one and half a dozen of the other", "A bit of a barney", "On the same wavelength/on different wavelengths", also, often heard in political negotiations, "Open and frank discussion".

- **Debating Society**
  For this rather formal activity you really need a group of at least five people, divided into two teams of two, plus at least one person to be an audience and voter. Ideally you would also have a chairperson, but this may not be possible and as long as people use good conversational rules you should be able to manage.

  Someone (chosen by the toss of a coin?) picks a debatable subject and begins with "This House believes ..." and states the team's opinion. The opposing team states their opinion, then a series of reasons, developments of the ideas and counter-arguments are given in an orderly manner from each side. Turn-taking and politeness are important. After a set length of time each team must sum up their argument and reasoning and the 'audience' must vote for the winner.

- **Mediation**
  This exercise relates to the Debating Society activity. Three people are needed: two opponents and one mediator. The opponents are given a topic about which they must pretend to have different, but strongly held, opinions. These are just scenarios to practise so the opinions are not their own.

  The topics could be about, say, whether school uniforms should be banned; whether successful weight loss diets should be rewarded by local government;

whether fly-tipping in the countryside, discarding rubbish in a city street, allowing dogs to foul pavements and so on, should attract much heavier punishment; whether archaeological digs should take place before the start of any new building projects; whether we should all have one day a week when we take nutritional substitutes rather than eat any food; whether pocket money should be at a standard rate for all children and so on.

To begin, the mediator asks each opponent in turn to state their side of the argument. Then he asks each one to state what they understand the other person's opinion to be. The third stage is to ask each opponent to state how they might make a slight compromise. Finally they must make a plan to agree in such a way that both are satisfied. Once everyone has had a turn at opposing as well as mediating in a hypothetical scenario it's a good idea to practise arguing real ideas but from the perspective of a person holding the opposite opinion from yours. Finally try out real opinions on personal beliefs but maintain the rules and be polite. It's recommended that you choose lightweight topics rather than anything to do with religion or politics.

ARGUMENT, MAKING A POINT AND DETACHMENT FROM YOUR OPINIONS

Argument, making a point and detachment from your opinions 'credit cards' for homework

> Today I'm going to watch an argument in a TV 'soap' or other drama. I'll see how and why the argument develops, make a note of it and bring my thoughts to the next group session.

> Today I'm going to try to observe differences of opinion between work colleagues/other students and see why they do or do not develop into arguments.

> Today I'm going to listen to an argument in a radio 'soap' or other drama. I'll consider how and why the argument develops, make a note of it and bring my thoughts to the next group session.

> Today I'm going to try to observe differences of opinion between work colleagues/other students and chip in with my own opinions, but in a way that does not escalate the disagreement by using a 'detaching phrase'.

> Today I'm going to watch or listen to a difference of opinion in a TV or radio interview or discussion programme. I'll see how and why the argument develops, make a note of it and bring my thoughts to the next group session.

> Today I'm going to try to observe a developing argument at home. I'll try to act as mediator, but will have to remember that they don't know the formal rules of negotiating in this way.

APOLOGIES AND REPAIRING CONVERSATIONAL 'GAFFES'

24

Self-assessment questionnaire

On a scale of 1–10, where 1 is very uncomfortable and 10 is perfectly comfortable, how do you feel about apologising and repairing conversational 'gaffes' and how do you cope if someone makes a conversational blunder against you? This could be something such as calling you the wrong name. How easy is this skill with the following types of people:

- *family members?*
- *one close friend?*
- *a group of friends?*
- *a new person in a formal situation such as an interview?*

People sometimes need to apologise for behavioural mistakes such as being late, forgetting a birthday and so on, but this chapter considers conversational blunders and how, by using repair strategies, we can do more than apologise.

Do you find it irritating when someone makes a conversational blunder? This could be something as simple as calling you by the wrong name. Family members often do this inadvertently and usually such mistakes are best ignored. The blunders are excused because the household is a place where attention and focus on talk is compromised by the need to get on with daily tasks, often in a hurry.

However, if you are at an interview for a job and the interviewer calls you by the wrong name it will be important to mention it the first time they do it so that you are not at cross purposes and so that if you get the job just in case there is an interviewee with the other name!

Similarly if you are introduced to a group of people by your friend who has momentarily had a blank moment and called you the wrong name it will be important to correct it right from the start, but make a joke of it otherwise your friend will be embarrassed.

Your task in the above situations is to distinguish between harmless and potentially harmful gaffes, so that you can decide when to ignore the mistake and when to make a repair.

Have you ever felt silenced or awkward because of the need to avoid certain topics of conversation? So much so that you mentioned the very thing you were trying to avoid? My grandmother used to recall a moment in her childhood when her mother had warned that a lady was coming to lunch and that she (grandma) must on no account mention the large wart on the visitor's nose. All went well until pudding was served, at which point the mother asked the visitor if she would like some custard on her wart! Grandma suppressed her laughter while her mother cringed with embarrassment. There is no record of the visitor's reaction.

Picture a situation where someone asks whether you'd like to go out shopping/come for coffee/a party when you have just told them that you are going to a funeral that day. The blunder is probably caused because they hadn't paid attention or have a poor memory rather than by insensitivity. In this case it's best to put the other person at ease about their blunder by gently pointing out their mistake. They will probably feel bad enough anyway about their gaffe when they realise it, so there's no need to make things worse by getting cross or looking insulted.

On the other hand, you might be the one making the mistake, for example, having asked someone when the baby is due only to find she's not pregnant, but just put on weight! Would this make you cringe with embarrassment? A quick apology, acknowledgement of your mistake, humour, self-deprecation and/or appreciation of their feelings are usually the best remedies. Apply one or two of them as soon as possible.

Remember that everyone makes blunders in conversations from time to time, the mistakes are just that – not intentional. If we were all so focused on saying the right thing without a single mistake, choosing and weighing every word with care, then free relaxed conversation would never take place. Don't dwell on your blunder after the conversation has finished. They will probably have forgotten it.

Do you ever watch outtakes and bloopers from movies or TV shows? If so you will realise that the actors are able to laugh at their own and each other's mistakes without blame, embarrassment or annoyance because everybody makes mistakes sometimes. The bloopers are endearing rather than annoying.

One of the presenters of BBC Radio 4's 'Today' programme has an effective method for self-correction of mistakes that he makes when giving an interviewee's name or details. He coughs straight away to cover up by diverting the listeners' attention away from the gaffe and towards the cough.

A note about blunders coming from children. They are inclined to be blunt in their comments and to state facts straightforwardly, such as: "You don't have your girlfriend any more." Don't feel aggrieved about this sort of thing, they are not trying to be judgemental or hurtful, but are just acknowledging your current situation and might even be trying to help.

Try these exercises

- **Miss Nomer**
  Give each person in the group a new name which is written on a label to be worn as a badge. The first scenario is a meeting between two work colleagues. Choose one person to be the 'repairer' while another group member becomes the 'blunderer' who greets the name on the label but uses the wrong name. First try a wrong name that sounds a bit similar to the name on the badge, so if the correct name is Marcus call him Mark or Matthew. The repairer must now correct the blunderer just by saying the proper name and smiling as if excusing the mistake. Now the blunderer calls him a completely different name such as Fred and the repairer says his name a bit more forcefully, so "Actually I'm Marcus" would be appropriate. Still smile though. Each have a turn or two as the repairer and as the blunderer.

  Second scenario – an interview for a job in an office. Here the blunderers will be the interviewers. Let's say the interviewee's name is John Dean, but the interviewer greets him as Jack Dee, James Dean or John Dorey for example. The repairer needs to correct this mistake politely, and wait for a few moments while the interviewer adjusts his paperwork and begins again. Again, each group member should have a turn as the interviewer who blunders and as the interviewee who repairs.

  The third scenario, still using the badges, is a friendly social gathering where a friend introduces you to a group, but uses the wrong name. This is awkward as he's your friend and you don't want to embarrass him, but at the same time you need all these new people to use your correct name. Discuss and try out the best way to solve this problem and each take a turn to be wrongly named. You could also try a variation on this game where you use your real names, that is, without the badges, but the blunderer still calls you the wrong name.

- **Oops!**
  You will need photos of people for this. Take them from newspapers, magazines or Speechmark cards but, to avoid misunderstandings, don't do this as a circle game. Give each image a name which you write on a piece of paper and attach with a paperclip.

Now one participant makes a conversational blunder towards an image while another acts out a response as if they were actually the person depicted. They will both act as repairers to the original mistake:

Let's assume you have a photo of a woman wearing a jumper. The blunderer might say: "Oh, how nice, you've worn your lovely comfy jumper again." The jumper-wearer character responds with: "Actually I bought this one yesterday." The blunderer could then say: "Sorry, I'd be hopeless as a fashion editor wouldn't I?", add a smile and a laugh, and then add: "Anyway, this one really suits you." The jumper-wearer might add: "Oh, don't worry at all, I know the one you mean and it is a bit similar."

A similar scenario to be acted out might involve someone asking whether a person has had a good holiday in Spain, whereas the holiday was actually in Italy. Someone could ask how the house decorating is going, whereas it was actually that the house was being sold. Perhaps ask how the new job is going whereas in fact the person has just become unemployed. It's important to use potentially sensitive topics as these might be the ones most needed in a real-life situation and it's comforting to know that you have practised coping with something similar, either as the maker of the blunder or as the recipient of it.

Apologies and repairing conversational 'gaffes' 'credit cards' for homework

> Today I'm going to listen for gaffes and repairs made in radio or TV interviews with celebrities or politicians. I'll make a note of them and discuss them at the next group session.

> Today I'm going to listen for gaffes and repairs made in radio or TV plays or 'soaps'. I'll make a note of them and discuss them at the next group session.

> Today I'm going to try to find misprints and typos in newspapers. I'll also look for any apologies for more serious mistakes the journalists have made in a previous article. I'll bring them along for discussion at the next group session.

> Today I'm going to listen for conversational blunders made by other people during a coffee break at a café/work/university/school or by eavesdropping on people on a bus.

> Today I'll tell my family I'm working on conversational gaffes – I'll warn them I'll be calling them the wrong name and they are not to be offended. I'll wait until they are not expecting it, call them the wrong name, deal with the consequences and remind them this was a practice.

> Today I'll tell my family I'm working on conversational gaffes and I'll be making a deliberate blunder. I'll think of a light-hearted gaffe, use it when they are not expecting it, deal with the consequences and remind them that this was just for practice.

ESCAPING!

Self-assessment questionnaire

On a scale of 1–10, where 1 is awkward and 10 is perfectly comfortable, how do you feel about politely closing a conversation and getting away from:

- just one friend who you meet on the street when you are in a hurry to catch a bus?
- a member of your family chatting at home when you want to go out to meet some friends?
- a person on their own chatting to you at a party when you want to talk to some friends you haven't seen for ages?
- an elderly neighbour who always pops out and tries to engage you in a lengthy conversation when you want to get home?
- a phone call from someone you like, but who is a 'rambler'?
- an ex-girlfriend/boyfriend who keeps phoning or chatting to you at work/university/school?
- a telephone salesperson?
- a friend or family member who keeps chatting once the film has started?

Have a look at and discuss the last quotation from the chapter called 'Sayings and points to consider about conversations' (see page 162) where James Nathan Miller is quoted as saying that: "There is no such thing as a worthless conversation, provided you know what to listen for."

The point is that almost all attempts at conversation from other people should be given time and attention. Try to think of each conversation as a 'mini relationship' where it is generally considered well-mannered to extricate yourself in a way that leaves the other person feeling pleased to have spoken to you and won't leave them feeling rejected when you go. Your conversation partner may also feel the need to close the conversation and in that case it's best not to keep adding extra topics, and not to feel rejected; they need to move on just as you do.

A standing-up social gathering

It is a difficult social skill to balance your wish to move away from a conversation partner with a need to retain the 'social grace' of staying with them. However, it is perfectly understandable to feel that a conversation has run its course and that you would like to move on.

There are some precautions you can take before a conversation begins in order to smooth your exit path. In the scenario of a social gathering indoors try to avoid being physically 'boxed into' the corner of a room, that is, two sides blocked by walls and the other two blocked by people. Ideally, position yourself between the centre of the room and the doorway to another room so that you can easily move away. Have your glass only slightly filled so that you will soon need to recharge it, but again only put a little in, so that you can move on again with an: "Excuse me; I need to top up my drink." These two precautions will allow you to circulate more freely.

To play the numbers game for a moment, let's say the average length of time for a chat-based social evening is about three hours, that is, 180 minutes. That means you can talk to 18 people for a maximum of about 10 minutes each or 36 people for about five minutes, minus the time taken off for drink refills and so on. If there are more people than that you will either need to spend less time with each person or focus your main chats with fewer people. That's just the mechanics though; in reality you need to be aware of natural breaks in the conversation, the other person's need to move on, a good friend's appearance nearby so that you can move away smoothly. At this point it's best to excuse yourself to go and get a refill of your drink. If you want to leave an individual without leaving them stranded alone it's a good idea to introduce them to another person and then once they get talking it's time to move gently away, using the drink-refill tip.

A sitting-down occasion

If the social gathering is a sit-down meal you are probably going to be restricted to the same neighbours at the table all evening. If you get the opportunity to choose where to sit try to be central so that you have more people within easy speaking distance; that way you'll have a choice of conversation partners. At one dining table if there are more than six people the conversation will tend to split, so if you are central you'll be able to chip in to conversations on either side of you, without much effort at a transition strategy to move from one conversation to the other. Make sure the person you have been speaking to has finished their point, then agree but become quiet after that – another person may pick up their point. Now you can join in with the chat on your other side.

An unexpected knock at the door

It's nice to have visitors but no one has a right to impose themselves on you uninvited and it can be difficult to convey that you would rather not have them in for very long. I have a friend who recommends putting a coat on if there is an unexpected knock at the door. If the caller turns out to be a pleasant surprise visit from a friend she mentions that she has just come in, and can then invite the friend in. If on the other hand the visitor is not someone she wants to talk to at that moment she says she is just going out! I don't recommend that particular deception as things can go wrong and you could be caught out. A better alternative, if you don't want to see the person for a long conversation at that moment, is to restrict the chat to the doorstep or hallway; act as if pleased but surprised to see them and request to set up a proper meeting at another time as you are committed to doing something else just now (or possibly that you need to go out soon).

Meeting someone unexpectedly in the street
Chance meetings are good news because it's likely that the other person has just as good a reason to move on as you do. The best quick conversation is one where a greeting is hearty followed by a couple of 'Opening gambit'-type comments with short questions and responses, such as: "How are you?", "Isn't it a lovely/windy/horrible day?" Then there's usually a comment about why you are there at that time: "I'm on my way to the station/I'm nipping in to the Post Office" and so on. Give them time to respond, then say: "Lovely to see you, let's meet again when we have more time to chat" and then add a quick: "I'm sorry, I need to dash, bye for now but see you soon."

Conversational closures
There is an art to 'conversational closures' and a typical occasion when this technique will be needed is when a phone call turns into a marathon. This partly happens because there are no body language cues or clues to help you indicate that you need to hurry up. You can protect yourself from known 'phone call ramblers' if you are the one making the call, by starting with "Just a quick call …". If you are the one answering the call you can try your usual greeting for that person, but add something at the start to indicate that you haven't got very much time to talk because you have an appointment, are going out and so on.

During the conversation, if it is lasting longer than you would like, you can try some 'winding down' statements. Try "OK, so … (recap main point of conversation)", "Well, thanks for all that information" or "So glad to hear your news, that's great." Then add a more obvious closing statement such as: "Thanks for phoning", "Lovely to talk to you, sorry I have to go, but let's catch up again soon" or "I'd better not keep you/I'd better let you go, I know you are busy." If absolutely desperate, as a last resort you could try "Oh, must go, there's someone at the door."

Try these exercises

- **Hello Goodbye Circle**
  The first participant greets the next and begins to talk or looks as if they are waiting for a conversation to start. The next participant responds with a greeting but ends the conversation politely and as quickly as possible, and then greets the next player in the circle who must in turn finish the conversation quickly. Each goodbye procedure must be different from the last.

- **Closing Body Language**

    This is a silent version of the previous exercise. One person shows enthusiastic 'Pleased to meet you' body language, the next indicates by body language only that they are too busy to talk/don't feel in the mood for a chat/are on their way somewhere and must hurry. Continue around the circle and discuss which facial expressions, postures and gestures go with conversation closure.

- **Escape Scenarios**

    You will need two people to act out each scenario and each person needs to have a try at being the conversational escapee.

    - *Friends meet on the street in a busy town. One wants to chat but the other is in a hurry to catch a bus.*

    - *A parent is chatting at home to their young adult child who wants to go out to meet some friends.*

    - *At a party a person is looking forward to talking to some valued friends not seen for ages. However, the friends are on the opposite side of the crowded room and another person is not only blocking the way but beginning to chat.*

    - *An elderly person pops out and tries to engage their next-door neighbour in yet another lengthy conversation just as they are wearily returning from work/a shopping trip.*

    - *A person at home has five minutes before their favourite TV programme starts. There is a phone call from someone who is a friend, but also a 'rambler'.*

    - *A person at home has five minutes before their favourite TV programme starts. There is an unwanted phone call from a double-glazing salesperson.*

    - *A person at work/university/school feels pestered by an ex-girlfriend/boyfriend who keeps phoning or chatting during the working day.*

    - *A person watching a film keeps being distracted by their friend/family member who keeps talking.*

    - *A person extricates themselves from a party.*

    - *Draw a meeting, or this SLT session, to a close.*

ESCAPING!

Escaping! 'credit cards' for homework

> Today I'm going to listen to an interview on the TV or radio and notice how the presenter draws the interview to a close.

> Today I'm going to watch or listen to a TV or radio drama and look out for styles of conversation closure. I'll make a note of them and bring them in for discussion.

> Today, just for fun, I'll research the 'famous last words' of one or more well-known people. I'll also try to think what my own light-hearted famous last words might be! I'll bring my ideas back for discussion.

> Today I'll phone a friend who is a 'rambler' and start by mentioning this is a quick call. When the chat seems too long I'll try a 'winding down' statement, close with "Lovely to talk to you/I'd better not keep you chatting any longer", await their response, repeat the cheerio and put the phone down.

> Today I'm going to try greeting a friend in the street, chatting for about two minutes, and then extricating myself politely.

> Today I'm going to try closing a conversation with a family member after about four minutes.

ELECTRONIC CONVERSATIONS   26

Self-assessment questionnaire

On a scale of 1–10, where 1 is very uncomfortable and 10 is perfectly comfortable, how do you feel about having a conversation by texting, emailing or Skyping and reporting on your activities by blog or twitter with:

- *members of your family?*
- *friends?*
- *authority figures?*
- *strangers?*

Many people who have difficulty with face-to-face conversations can more easily have social interactions by electronic means. This is a great way for them to add to their communication possibilities. You may well be familiar with these forms of communication and know the advantages and pitfalls associated with them, and the etiquette needed to use them well. If you are fully acquainted with all of this then move swiftly on or have just a brief look and carry out some of the homework tasks.

Emails

As with other forms of communication, there are good manners and rules to follow if you use email. Most importantly, although emails are generally less formal than letters, you still need to make the effort to reply because people can be offended if you don't respond.

Emails written for business purposes will tend to have more formal beginnings and endings than emails to friends and family. Formal emails usually begin with "Dear …". Casual emails often begin without any formal salutation, or just "Hi", especially if the email is one of a series. Please see the chapter on 'Formal and casual conversations' for more detail on style. Correct spelling, use of capital letters and punctuation are not quite so important in a casual email, however, sometimes writers of emails are in such a hurry that the email becomes difficult to understand, so it's definitely worth checking, just briefly, that your email will be clear.

A few extra points:
- Do restrict email conversations to about four connected comments and keep the same label throughout that series, so that each writer can look back through their mails to find those on a particular subject, for example, four connected comments

about a planned outing are fine, but if you also want to communicate with that person about, say, Christmas presents, you should start a separate chain of email comments so that information doesn't get forgotten or lost.

- Keep emails short. If you have a lot to say on a subject, want to include a list or any extra document that the recipient might want to keep, it's usually best to send it as an attachment.

- Use spaced paragraphs or bullet points to make the email easy to read.

- Use a formal font if the recipient is a formal person.

Text messages

The text message is a good way to keep in touch with people who you like to make quick contact with on most days. A text message doesn't interrupt someone's working day in the way a phone call does; the recipient can answer when it suits them. However, as with emails, it is important that a reply is made because people can feel snubbed if they are ignored.

Most texts are informal in style; rules can often be slightly relaxed regarding the use of capital letters and punctuation, and acronyms are frequent.

The new generation of smartphones can easily take, send and receive photos, so these can be included in the message to bring to life much more detail for the recipient.

Emoticons are frequently used to enhance a message. Take a careful look at the array of them because there are often more relevant examples than just the smiley or sad faces. I know of a couple who text each other almost entirely with emoticons and photos, with almost no words at all, because they find it a more intuitive and fun way to communicate.

Texts are useful for making quick requests, for example, not to forget the milk, when the recipient is at the supermarket. In 'textese', this message can be abbreviated to 'dont 4get milk'.

To give a brief reminder that you hope it's still arranged that you'll see the person at the café at 2 o'clock this afternoon you might text 'c u 2pm cafe ok?'

Plan what you are going to include in a text message, because brevity is the key to quick, speech-like exchanges. Make use of acronyms to save time; frequently used examples are omg (oh my god), cul8r (see you later), 1derfl (wonderful), gr8 (great). There is also lol, which is one acronym that causes trouble, because some people think it means 'lots of love', whereas the agreed meaning has become 'laugh out loud'. So a text message saying 'uncle billy broke leg, in hospital lol fred' would be unfortunate!

A word of warning about text messages; they have unfortunately become a vehicle for spreading rumours and for bullying and abuse. If you receive a bullying text message you should not reply to it. Don't delete it though; it's best to log it as evidence should you need to make a formal complaint. Sometimes cyberbullying by text takes the form of 'sexting'. This involves sending or receiving inappropriate and explicit text messages and images. For more information about how to avoid this form of cyberbullying please see the CEOP link on page 142, just before 'Try these exercises'. Above all never suffer any abuse in silence – let a trusted person know that this is happening to you.

Social networking

Social networking sites such as Facebook and LinkedIn serve several purposes:

Facebook is largely informal. You may want to use it to communicate directly or to update your status, or to broadcast information about yourself more generally to your Facebook friends. Take care though; you may find that more people are aware of information about you than you had planned, so only put on the site things that you are happy for everyone to know. Be careful with any photos you place on your Facebook pages – do you really want your family or your boss to see you drunk? Be sure to look at and change privacy settings if your current ones are too accessible.

LinkedIn can be thought of as a professional form of Facebook in which your CV can be included and updated, and other information, such as work you have carried out and articles and so on that you have had published, is noted and can be seen by potential employers and colleagues.

Google plus operates a model of concentric circles of friendship, with the closest friends at the centre and progressively less close friends in the outer circles. This way you can decide who sees which information by their degree of familiarity. Facebook has copied this idea and is now retrospectively implementing this so you are obliged to categorise into family, close friends, acquaintances and so on.

Chat rooms can be a way to practise conversing with strangers. These are to be used with caution. Most importantly, never give out your phone or address details in a chat room. I do not recommend setting up dates via the internet, but if you do make an arrangement to meet a person in this way I strongly advise you to take a friend with you, the first time you meet, and always let another person know where and when your meeting is arranged.

Twitter If you join Twitter your 'tweets' need to be kept short (currently 140 characters although this may change). Twitter is a good way of sharing information and opinions but remember that your tweets can be seen by even more people, including strangers, so be careful what you write.

Blogs This word is an abbreviated form of 'web log' and, as the name suggests, is a log, or diary, which could be used to broadcast your thoughts, your recipes (as in the film Julie and Julia, 2009) or other information. It is usually updated regularly; you can choose whether to update daily, weekly, monthly and so on. Again be aware that others, apart from your expected target readers, can see your information, so be careful about writing things that might upset people and could cause them to sue you if you say something rude or untrue about them. The 'Blogosphere' is written from a personal perspective, but accessible to the general public.

Instant messaging, such as MSN, Skype or Facetime, takes place in real time, just as a normal conversation, so previous conversation strategies apply. Nowadays Skype is often used for business conferencing, as a means of saving expense and time on travel. (It has largely superseded video conferencing.) Skype involves the presence of video cameras, often built in to new laptops and smartphones, so skills to do with body language (especially facial expression) need to be remembered, and you need to be sure that you, or whatever image you are trying to show, can be seen by the camera. With MSN there can be a combination of words and emoticons but without the addition of photos or the extra clues given by voice you need to be aware of the meanings of the emoticons.

Note: Cyberbullying can take place online, via text messages and through other electronic means. The key strategy to avoid this is to keep your personal information private. Find out much more from the CEOP website's latest initiative www.thinkuknow.co.uk much of which applies to all ages, not only children.

Try these exercises

- **1derful**

    Many abbreviations for text messages involve substituting a number for some letters, as in l8r (later). Each member of the group could try making a list of words that could be made using number substitutions and exchange them with others in the group to make sure everyone understands every example. Here are a few to get the group started: 1derful, 2bular, 4est. Now make whole sentences in this way.

    A funny extension to this game, just for fun, is the '+1' variation. For this you each try to make a sentence using as many number substitutions as possible but adding 1 to each number, so that 2day becomes 3day, for example: '3day I 2der whether 3 go 5 a walk in the 5est.' This is just for fun and to encourage lateral thinking, not for real use.

- **Broadcast or Secret**
  Discuss which pieces of information are appropriate for which kinds of people to know and which latest pieces of your news, in words and/or images, you are happy to broadcast to all. Would you be happy for your boss or teacher to see images of you cavorting on the beach on a day when you called in sick? Are you happy for all members of your family to be included in your holiday images?

- **Emoticons**
  Enlarge and print out an array of emoticons and stick them on to cards to be used for games such as Snap and Pelmanism. Play those games in the group; also try copying the faces then discuss their meanings and say which ones apply to you at this moment.

Electronic conversations 'credit cards' for homework

Today I'm going to text a quick comment about the weather or an event to a friend/family member, using as many abbreviations as possible but still being clear.

Today I'm going to text a request or arrangement to meet to a friend/family member, using abbreviations but still being clear.

Today I'll write two emails: a casual note to a friend and a formally worded email to a Tourist Office requesting information about events or accommodation. I'll print them and bring them to the next SLT session.

Today I'm going to watch either the film *The Social Network* about the origins of Facebook or *Julie and Julia* about the power of blogs. Both are available as DVDs.

Today I'm going to investigate the idea of joining a social network and/or setting up a blog. I'll bring my ideas and decision to the next group meeting.

Today I'm going to investigate the idea of joining Twitter and also see whether I could start Skyping my friends. I'll bring my ideas and decision to the next group meeting.

EAVESDROPPING

27

Self-assessment questionnaire

On a scale of 1–10, where 1 is dubious/uncomfortable and 10 is perfectly comfortable, how do you feel about listening in to other people's chat when you are:

- alone on the bus or train and someone is speaking loudly on their mobile phone?
- alone on the bus or train and some rowdy football supporters are joking with each other?
- alone on the bus or train and people are talking to each other in normal or slightly quiet voices?
- at a social gathering and you are in one group but you are distracted by and can easily hear the chat of another group?
- (a) alone and (b) with one friend at a restaurant where the tables are rather close together and people at the next table are talking?
- in department store or motorway restrooms where people often arrive in pairs?
- outside a room in which people are having a meeting?
- also, how do you feel if you find someone eavesdropping on you?

This chapter adds to 'Choosing and introducing a conversation topic'. Eavesdropping is an area that needs to be looked at from both sides: that of the listener and that of the person overheard.

A rich source of conversation topics can be found when you overhear other, unknown people talking, for example, when you are standing in a queue or sitting in front of them on the bus, train or plane. The topics are usually personal, non-political small talk and will be heard in snippets rather than complete finished dialogues. They are sometimes very funny and quotable.

It's an easy homework task to see how many potential conversation topics you can pick up and how many comments you can quote just by eavesdropping. Once you are tuned in to the task you'll even be able to overhear something worthwhile as you walk along a busy high street. There are also opportunities to observe the way in which people interact with their children, friends or partners and to decide whether to imitate or avoid those ways of talking.

In my opinion any loudly held conversation on a mobile phone, for example, on a train, is fair game for eavesdroppers and the collection of quotable quotes is compensation for the irritation of having to listen. I have learned in this way about pay rates for secretaries in London, various business plans and what time a dinner party was going to take place and what the menu was. I once overheard two women talking about the need to collect conkers to put in the corners of rooms to counter spider invasions! (By the way, I've now tried it and it does seem to work, what a gem of an eavesdrop that was!)

Lynda Barry, American cartoonist and author, said in an interview: "I listen like mad to any conversation taking place next to me just trying to hear why this is funny. Women's restrooms are especially great. I wash my hands twice waiting for people to come in and start talking."

Nigel Rees, who devised and hosts the very funny Radio 4 panel game programme 'Quote Unquote' has written a book called *Eavesdroppings. Bizarre Overheard Remarks* which is full of interesting and hilarious things people have heard. Borrow this book from a library if you can to see the kind of remarks that you might use to enhance conversation. It's even better to collect your own examples rather than using those in the book.

Collecting anonymous quotes like this is fine and may add to your future conversation topics. A key point to remember is not to give any sign that you are listening in. If people become aware that they are being overheard they will often clam up.

The down side of eavesdropping is when the overheard person is known to the eavesdropper and the words are quoted maliciously. Imagine if someone were to overhear you quietly talking to your close friend or family member about issues to do with your health, your disappointments or your love life. It would be hurtful and humiliating to have this information passed around. Equivalent to that, and therefore definitely to be avoided, would be reading letters, texts or emails intended for someone else, or listening in to someone's private and quiet phone calls. Linked to this, a few notorious cases of 'hacking into' other people's phone calls and emails have taken place in recent years and been reported in newspapers. This kind of behaviour can compromise the safety and dignity of people and organisations. Never do it.

Try these exercises

- **Comparing Notes**
  Compare notes about things the group members have overheard that have amused or taught something new. This exercise should be repeated once several of the homework tasks have been completed.

  When the group has had some opportunities to collect a few examples of eavesdropping discuss what proportion of them seem to be bits of advice, comments about food, pay, clothes, prices, nice or nasty comments about other people and so on.

- **Parallel Conversations**
  Try having two parallel conversations going on at the same time in two separate parts of the room or at two tables. The task is to participate in the conversation at your table, but try to pick up snippets from the conversation at the other table.

- **Overhearing Top Secrets**
  Discuss what could go wrong if you overhear a formal conversation about, say, company policy while you are outside the boss's office waiting for the right moment to knock and collect something.

- **Chinese Whispers**
  You need at least five people really to play the game of Chinese whispers. One person whispers a phrase or sentence into the ear of the person next to them, who whispers what they heard into the next person's ear and so on around the table until the final person repeats what he heard. This game is improved if the participants who are not the active whisperer or listener mumble to each other, or say "rhubarb, rhubarb, rhubarb" continually until it is their turn to listen or whisper. Usually, the final statement will be significantly different from the original. Discuss how something heard as a result of eavesdropping, just as much as a Chinese whisper, can be misheard, passed on incorrectly, misheard again and generally undergo a transformation.

- **Off the Record**
  Discuss whether it is fair for reporters to quote the comments made by politicians who believed themselves to be speaking privately away from a microphone. Are these quotes by reporters in any way comparable to the kinds of photos taken by paparazzi of celebrities who thought they were having private moments?

Eavesdropping 'credit cards' for homework

> Today, without being noticed, I'm going to try to overhear the chat of another passenger on public transport. I'll make a note of it and report back to the SLT session.

> Today, without being noticed, I'm going to try to overhear the chat of someone in a queue at a supermarket. I'll make a note of it and report back to the SLT session.

> Today, without being noticed, I'm going to try to overhear the chat of other people at a café table near mine. I'll make a note of it and report back to the SLT session.

> Today, without being noticed, I'm going to listen out for loudly held mobile phone conversations. I'll make a note of them and report back to the SLT session.

> Today I'm going to borrow a copy of one of the 'Quote Unquote' books and have a look at the 'Eavesdroppings' sections.

> Today I'm going to watch a film and listen for two examples of eavesdropping. What effect do the overheard words have on the listener's behaviour? I'll bring my thoughts to the next session.

CONVERSATION AT PARTIES AND SPECIAL OCCASIONS

Self-assessment questionnaire

On a scale of 1–10, where 1 is difficult and 10 is easy, how do you feel about adjusting your conversational style according to a particular occasion (depending on which apply to you), for example, at:

- *a party with a group of friends?*
- *a family gathering?*
- *a birthday party at a nightclub?*
- *a works Christmas party?*
- *an end-of-college/university farewell party or school prom?*
- *a Valentine's Day party?*

In a way, this chapter sums up most of the previous chapters. At a party you'll need many of the skills you have worked on, and there are a few extras worth considering.

The kind of chat you have with friends and new people at a party will not be the same as a conversation at a family gathering. This chapter looks at the adjustments that need to be made when anticipating types of conversations at various locations and venues.

Before a party you may be worrying about receiving invitations, preferring not to go to any social occasions for fear of saying the wrong thing. Perhaps you look back at previous parties and sense that they did not go well for you. Or perhaps you feel that you have missed out on the enjoyment of these social gatherings and want to gather up some basic tips and suggestions for future occasions. Here are a few basic tips and confidence-building suggestions for those who may feel doubtful about going to parties.

Try these exercises

- **Miss Nomer**
  Have a group chat about the advantages of attending parties, the point of having fun, the point of meeting new people and refreshing old friendships.

- **Research the Party**

    Discuss how much more confident you will feel if you understand what type of event the party will be, what it involves and how to prepare for it. It's often worthwhile thinking the prospective party scene through beforehand, much as a sportsperson imagines their exact movements before their event. They imagine all the moves going well, of course, and this is wise for you at your occasion too.

- **Last Time**

    Try to remember how you felt about the last party you attended. Before the party what did you anticipate going wrong? How many of those things actually happened? Exchange your thoughts with others in the group.

The invitation

- **Preparation**

    Imagine you have been given a written invitation. Look at it carefully. Is it to be a small gathering of friends or a large works event? Are there instructions about what to wear, for example, is 'Fancy Dress' mentioned? Is the party at someone's house, at work, at a smart hotel or informally, at a pub? If the invitation was spoken and you now feel unclear about the details, you might want some clarification. What sorts of questions might you ask the person who invited you?

- **Presents**

    Is the party the type of event where a present ought to be given to the host/hostess? Should you contribute a bottle of wine or other drink?

- **Mock-Ups**

    Here are some mock-ups of invitation types. Print them all out, one copy for each group member. For each occasion consider what you would wear and what you would bring. People often forget to include important information so consider whether there is anything you need to clarify/ask about. Jot down your answers and list anything you might need to buy. Compare everyone's answers.

    - Pinned on the notice board:

        Works Christmas Dinner, lunchtime Tuesday 20th December in the Canteen. All welcome.

CONVERSATION AT PARTIES AND SPECIAL OCCASIONS

- A note included in a Christmas card:

  Please come to our New Year's party!! Contributions gratefully received. Steve and Emma.

- A gold-edged card sent by post:

  You are cordially invited to the Company Christmas Party

  Royal George Hotel

  Tuesday 20th December 8pm

- Sent by group email:

  Hi all,
  We're having a party in honour of Faith's 25th birthday. It's a 'James Bond' theme. See you on Saturday, 8pm at our house.

- Part of a chat at work or at college:

  … As it's nearly Christmas, some of us are meeting at the pub on Friday. Would you like to come?

- A message left on your phone:

  Hi Hannah, Just to say hope you can come to the party next week? I'm going, would you like a lift?

Arriving

- **Discuss**
  Discuss which of the above events would need you to arrive on time and which are the types when people tend to arrive slightly later than stated on the invitation. Is it ever a good idea to arrive much earlier than the invitation states?

- **Party Role Play**
  Take the opportunity of the SLT setting to hone your party-going skills. Best of all would be to practise a whole party so that all skills can be practised in a fun way, but you might need to rehearse the individual skills first before putting them all together.

  Role play different ways to join the party. Take turns to be the host, the new arrival and the people at the party who have already established themselves into conversational pairings or groupings. Ideally you would have about eight people in the group for this exercise, although you can manage with five.

Depending on how you set things up, the 'host' can leave his guests to answer the door while the host continues chatting to people as the new guest arrives. If the host lets the new guest in, how long should they talk to each other? See what happens if the chat with the host is very short and how things vary when the chat goes on for too long. There are other guests for the host and the new arrival to consider.

- **First Contact**
  If you are the new guest and you enter the room alone you should take a short while to consider who to talk to; usually it's best to start with the host, especially if there is a gift or bottle to offer. If the host is busy the best initial conversation partner could be someone else who you already know or someone standing alone.

- **Eye the Guests**
  Practise making eye contact with people across a room as well as at the usual conversational distance (arm's length). Experiment with the size of smile needed for someone standing close to you and for someone standing on the other side of the room.

- **Not Enough Hands**
  Practise walking and holding a glass in a confident but relaxed way. Consider how you are going to manage a glass and a plate at the same time, and practise this too. In an SLT group you might have to make do with mugs and paper plates for the exercise, but it's still worth a practice!

Conversation for parties

- **Background Music**
  Practise talking to each other with and without music/background chatter. Discuss how we change volume according to background noise.

- **Keeping it Light**
  In the SLT group discuss which kinds of conversation will be best for a light-hearted social gathering like this. Which of these topics would be appropriate: a recent funny thing that happened to you? Politics? News of the royals? Your journey to the party? How you know the host? Your memories of the host's teenage antics? Something funny that you have heard on the news? Comments about the food, the

venue, the music? Also please look back at and recap the chapter on 'Choosing and introducing a conversation topic'.

- **Listen!**
  Be aware of the need to listen to what people have to say rather than overwhelming them with details about yourself and your interests. If they seem unforthcoming try asking them open questions – ones which require more than a one-word answer. Avoid 'bombarding' people with questions though.

- **Be Agreeable**
  Parties are not a time for arguments and it's best not to be remembered after the party as the grumpy one who kept disagreeing.

- **Surprises**
  'Conversational surprises' can perk up a flailing conversation. As long as you are with easy-going friends or family who are safe conversation groups/partners you can try a mock confrontation. This is done carefully, with a twinkle in the eye, to provoke a response when the conversation has become a bit dull. For example, you could say something slightly out of character such as: "I'm thinking of going on an all-chocolate diet", "I'm thinking of drumming up some support for a protest march in aid of … retired comedians" or "Hearing all the bad news this week, don't you think we should get rid of politicians/bankers/news programmes?"

  The conversational surprise could be a joke that you just introduce with a quick lead-in such as: "I heard this ever so funny joke" or "Have you heard this one?" For more tips on making jokes please see the chapter on 'Using humour'.

Circulating

- **Moving On**
  Usually, people talk with one group or individual for a while, then move on. Two main skills are needed – how to leave one situation and how to move into another.

- **Scenarios**
  Role play these scenarios:

  - *You want to leave a group. Excuse yourself to go and get a refill of your drink.*

  - *You want to leave an individual without leaving them stranded alone. Introduce them to another person and then use the drink-refill tip.*

- Join another group. Try standing nearby and smiling along with the chat. After a while add in a word or two.

Goodbyes

- **Don't Overstay**
    Generally it's better to leave a party with the guests wanting more of your company rather than having had too much of it. Role play preparing to leave by saying to other guests something like: "It's been a lovely evening, nice to meet you." Make sure you thank the host/hostess, say goodbye and then go.

Conversation at parties and special occasions 'credit cards' for homework

---

Today and over the next few days I'm going to re-read my homework cards from all the chapters in this book that I have worked on, and remember what we discussed. (They will all be useful preparation for a party.)

Today I'll turn on the radio and talk against it, quietly and then more loudly, experimenting with my voice against the radio volume. I'll also try listening to TV and radio discussions at the same time, and focus and retell one of the topics under discussion.

Today I'm going to watch the funny film *Hitch* (starring Will Smith), for extra hints about talking and dancing. I'll make notes for discussion in the group.

Today I'm going to make a list of parties and special events that I can remember attending and try to think back to the things that went well and the things I'd like to improve for another time.

Today I'm going to think about a forthcoming social event (even if it's a few weeks away). I'll practise my greetings and opening gambits, and introducing myself.

Today I'm going to buy a celebrity-type popular magazine containing party pictures and consider what people at those events might be discussing. I'll invent some likely topics, and bring the magazine and my ideas to the next SLT session.

THE CONVERSATION 'MENU'

29

This chapter aims to be a light-hearted discussion document, intended to be used towards the end of the course on improving conversation, for summing up everything that has been learned. There is no need for a self-assessment and no homework is required.

Do you enjoy food, in all its variety of presentations? Or do you regard it merely as a way of providing a set of nutritional needs – vitamins, minerals, carbohydrates, proteins and fats? In the same way, social exchanges can be enriching and enjoyable, rather than mere exchanges of information.

In food terms, social exchanges might be thought of like this:

- *A pleasant greeting is a bit like an enjoyable, but tiny piece of chocolate (a chocolate button).*

- *An extended greeting and 'opening gambit', which could include a brief enquiry about health or a mention of the weather, is like a cup of tea and a biscuit.*

- *A short chat is like a quick lunch of sandwiches and fruit.*

- *Eventually you reach the level of the full conversation, which is here compared with a full five-course meal.*

The Latin word *minutus* meant small. When it became a French word it evolved into 'menu' and referred to small details, then gradually became associated with the idea of the detailed list of items of a meal. A conversation, like a menu, can be broken down into courses and enjoyed a bit at a time. You would never have all the food presented on one plate: olives, soup, roast beef, ice cream, coffee and mints all chucked indigestibly together. In the same way, you need not worry about the whole conversation right at the beginning. Each course will tend to follow in order, so you don't need to worry that it will be too much to cope with, just tackle it a bit at a time.

Menu

Hors d'œuvres

Starters

Main Course with accompaniments, chef's special sauces etc or Today's Specials

Pudding

Coffee and mints

Throughout your meal – Wines to accompany

Conversation Menu

....

Hors d'œuvres

Smiles, greetings and enquiries about health.

....

Starters

Introductions of any new people to the group.

Exchanges of compliments.

Comments about the weather or the surroundings.

....

Main Course

Questions about the other people's partners/children/parents/'significant others' and a general catch-up on any information from the last conversation.

Selection of topics from people's news, often including each other's recent holidays.

Exchanges, and warm and friendly differences of opinion about current events.

'Today's Specials' would refer to special occasions such as someone's birthday or other celebration, so special comments, amusing reminiscences, expressions of appreciation would be included.

Pudding
Comments about films, TV programmes, theatre.
Exchange of each other's plans for next week or forthcoming events.

....

Coffee and mints
Positive statements about how much you have enjoyed the occasion and the company. Discussion and plans for next conversation – venue, time etc. These often begin with something like: "Hope to see you …".

....

Throughout your meal
At any point you can enjoy others' anecdotes and jokes or add your own. Remember to use the mechanics of conversing, taking turns, avoiding interrupting others (but sometimes having to put up with their interruptions!), using body language, asking and answering questions.

Try these exercises

- **The Full Menu**
  Write down a title to a recent full conversation you have had. It could be something like: 'A conversation with my neighbour after he returned from holiday', 'A long conversation over the phone with my cousin' or 'A conversation with my partner after a day at work.' Write down what you remember of the conversation and try to sort it approximately into the 'Conversation Menu'.

- **The Snack Menu**
  Think of your other recent social exchanges. Write them down and discuss with the group whether these conversations were 'chocolate buttons', 'a cup of tea and a biscuit' or 'sandwiches and fruit'.

- **Small Mouthfuls**
  Discuss how much better you feel about long conversations when they can be broken down in this way.

Bon Appetit!

SAYINGS AND POINTS TO CONSIDER ABOUT CONVERSATIONS

These are for consideration any time, perhaps at the end of a session when there are a few spare moments. Or you could add one to your homework to think about until the next session or have a copy to keep and ponder over whenever you like. Make notes in the margins to add your ideas.

- What is the point of chat? Is it right to call it 'idle gossip'?

- How do people seek regard through conversation?

- Why do people share confidences?

- Is a conversation a performance?

- What does 'capping your story' mean? How could capping someone's story annoy them?

- Is it important to win an argument?

- What could 'conversational code' mean?

- What is implied when a politician talks about "Open and frank discussions"?

- Somebody once said that: "Conversation shouldn't be throwing something at someone, more like throwing something to someone!" What did they mean?

- What could 'verbal duelling' mean?

- What does 'In the beginning was the word' mean? Where did it come from? Do you agree with it?

- What do these expressions mean? – 'between you and me'; 'he clammed up'; 'they go rabbiting on'; 'an awkward silence'; 'breaking the ice'; 'talking the hind leg off a donkey'.

- What did Winston Churchill mean when he said: "Jaw, jaw, not war, war."?

- It can be quite an effort to make conversation with someone or with several other people. Why is it worth it?

- What is a 'conversation piece'?

- What are 'talking heads'?

Finally, here are 12 quotations about conversation. Choose one which might be something for you to remember.

- *A conversation is a dialogue, not a monologue.* Truman Capote

- *Conversation between Adam and Eve must have been difficult at times because they had nobody to talk about.* Agnes Repplier

- *Love without conversation is impossible.* Mortimer Adler

- *Having a small number of guests is the only way to generate good conversation. Besides, your whole house doesn't get wrecked that way.* Paul Lynde

- *Saying what we think gives a wider range of conversation than saying what we know.* Cullen Hightower

- *Silence is one of the great arts of conversation.* Marcus Tullius Cicero

- *There is more than one right way to listen, to talk, to have a conversation – or a relationship.* Deborah Tannen

- *The great gift of conversation lies less in displaying it ourselves than in drawing it out of others. He who leaves your company pleased with himself and his own cleverness is perfectly well pleased with you.* Jean de la Bruyère

- *The reason why so few people are agreeable in conversation is that each is thinking more about what he intends to say than what others are saying.* François de La Rochefoucauld

- *The true spirit of conversation consists in building on another man's observation, not overturning it.* Edward G. Bulwer-Lytton

- *There is no conversation more boring than the one where everybody agrees.* Michel de Montaigne

- *There is no such thing as a worthless conversation, provided you know what to listen for. And questions are the breath of life for a conversation.* James Nathan Miller

Good Luck with your conversations and enjoy them!

APPENDIX 1: THE CONVERSATION STRATEGIES CHECKLIST: SELF-ASSESSMENT AND LOG

A journal of improvement

Strategy	Initial Score & Date	Date I observed others using this strategy / Comments	Date I used this strategy / Other comments	Final Score & Date
Greetings On a scale of 1–10, where 1 is difficult and 10 is easy, how do you feel about greeting: • just one friend of the same sex as you? • just one friend of the opposite sex? • a group of friends of the same sex as you? • a group of friends of the opposite sex or a mix of males and females? • new people in a familiar place, for example, at college/work? • new people not 'on your territory' – perhaps in a pub or a waiting room?				
Opening gambits On a scale of 1–10, where 1 is difficult and 10 is easy, how do you feel about making opening gambits with: • just one friend of the same sex as you? • just one friend of the opposite sex? • a group of friends of the same sex as you? • a group of friends of the opposite sex or a mix of males and females? • new people in a familiar place, for example, at college/work? • new people not 'on your territory' – perhaps in a pub or a waiting room?				

Strategy	Initial Score & Date	Date I observed others using this strategy Comments	Date I used this strategy Other comments	Final Score & Date
Introducing yourself On a scale of 1–10, where 1 is difficult and 10 is easy, how do you feel about introducing yourself to: • a peer of either sex? • other age groups (including children)? • authority figures?				
Remembering names On a scale of 1–10, where 1 is difficult and 10 is easy, how do you feel about: • remembering your conversation partner's name and using it during a social setting? • remembering and using the speaker's name quite often during a phone conversation? • remembering the name for the next time you meet?				
Mechanical rules On a scale of 1–10, where 1 is difficult and 10 is easy, how do you feel about following basic 'mechanical rules' of conversations such as: • being in the right place for a conversation? • understanding the conversation partner and asking for clarification? • avoiding interruptions (in both directions, ie where they interrupt you and where you find yourself interrupting them)?				

APPENDIX 1

Strategy	Initial Score & Date	Date I observed others using this strategy Comments	Date I used this strategy Other comments	Final Score & Date
• taking turns of the right length? • staying on the subject versus introducing a new topic? • linking your comment to the preceding one?				
Formulaic interchanges On a scale of 1–10, where 1 is difficult and 10 is easy, how do you feel about the everyday, brief, semi-social exchanges of words with the following people: • a shop assistant? • a person on the street who would like you to donate money for a good cause? • a person next to you in a long queue? • a fellow passenger on a train that has stopped for no apparent reason? • a waiter? • a taxi-driver? • your hairdresser/barber? • a pub landlord? • a member of staff at your bank – face to face, also by phone? • staff selling tickets at a cinema or theatre – face to face, also by phone? • a receptionist at a leisure centre or hotel – face to face, also by phone? • a person on the phone wanting to sell you double glazing?				

| Strategy | Initial Score & Date | Date I observed others using this strategy

Comments | Date I used this strategy

Other comments | Final Score & Date |
|---|---|---|---|---|
| **Formal and casual conversations**

On a scale of 1–10, where 1 is easy and 10 is difficult, how do you feel about recognising the differences between formal and casual conversation settings, and being able to use the right 'code' in the following situations:

- a barbecue party?
- a wedding?
- an interview?
- a fancy-dress party?
- a law court?
- a visit to the doctor?
- a visit to an elderly relative in hospital?
- a day out to a theme park?
- an open day at a college?
- a ceremony?
- a caution by the police?
- a chat with your sister's children?

Body language – expressing it

On a scale of 1–10, where 1 is difficult and 10 is easy, how do you feel about these aspects of body language:

- using eye contact with a friend as you greet them?
- using eye contact in a conversation – occasionally when you are the speaker | | | | |

APPENDIX 1

Strategy	Initial Score & Date	Date I observed others using this strategy / Comments	Date I used this strategy / Other comments	Final Score & Date
and frequently when you are the listener? • dividing your eye contact between a group of friends or colleagues? • smiling broadly as you greet your friend? • using facial expressions accurately? • using a faint smile as you greet anyone? • understanding and using gesture? • understanding and using posture? • shaking hands with somebody?				
Body language – interpreting it On a scale of 1–10, how do you feel about interpreting these aspects of body language in others: • noticing facial movements such as eyebrow position, openness of eyes, degree of smile, lips curling up or down, nose wrinkling, furrowing of forehead as in frowning? • matching facial expressions to emotions, for example: tears on a person's cheek; blushing; the surprise on the face of a person unexpectedly meeting a friend; shock when someone receives bad news? • understanding what is being conveyed by a hearty handshake? • interpreting the emotion felt by a small child stamping his foot? • interpreting uncontrollable giggling? • understanding the 'eyes met across a crowded room' scenario?				

Strategy	Initial Score & Date	Date I observed others using this strategy / Comments	Date I used this strategy / Other comments	Final Score & Date
- noticing and understanding: the shoulder shrug; hands on hips; folded arms; a drooping posture? - understanding the meaning of 'personal space'? - understanding what might be conveyed by a person's clothing/fashion choices?				
What are other people's interests? On a scale of 1–10, where 1 is difficult and 10 is easy, how do you feel about discovering your conversation partner's interests, when the person in question is: - a friend of the same sex as you? - a friend of the opposite sex? - a new acquaintance? - a potential new girlfriend/boyfriend?				
Open and closed questions, and invitations to speak On a scale of 1–10, where 1 is difficult and 10 is easy, how do you feel about asking social questions in a conversation with the following types of people: - a member of your family? - a friend? - a new person? - a prospective girlfriend/boyfriend? - a group of friends?				

APPENDIX 1

Strategy	Initial Score & Date	Date I observed others using this strategy — Comments	Date I used this strategy — Other comments	Final Score & Date
The www. technique On a scale of 1–10, where 1 is difficult and 10 is easy, how do you feel about keeping a conversation going with: • just one friend? • a group of friends? • a new person?				
Choosing and introducing a conversation topic On a scale of 1–10, where 1 is difficult and 10 is easy, how do you feel about choosing and introducing a topic with: • just one friend? • a mixed group of friends in a casual setting? • people from your workplace in a formal setting?				
Noticing, commenting and making polite observations On a scale of 1–10, where 1 is difficult and 10 is easy, how do you feel about noticing and commenting, that is, observing your surroundings or other people and making comments about them in the following types of situation: • a hotel, café, restaurant or pub? • a stately home, park or garden open to the public? • a religious building, museum or art gallery? • the high street in your local town?				

Strategy	Initial Score & Date	Date I observed others using this strategy Comments	Date I used this strategy Other comments	Final Score & Date
The Social CV On a scale of 1–10, where 1 is shy and 10 is confident, how do you feel about making use of your life experiences to add to the conversation with the following people: • just one friend? • a new friend of the opposite sex? • a mixed group of friends? • new people in a social setting? • colleagues in a workplace setting? • a barbecue party or a fancy-dress party? • a university or college open day? • a hospital? • a friend's house or garden?				
Using humour On a scale of 1–10, where 1 is difficult and 10 is easy, how do you feel about: • using humour with one friend? • using humour with a group of friends? • remembering and telling jokes? • using humorous self-deprecation? • using humorous anecdotes?				

APPENDIX 1

Strategy	Initial Score & Date	Date I observed others using this strategy / Comments	Date I used this strategy / Other comments	Final Score & Date
Compliments On a scale of 1–10, where 1 is difficult and 10 is easy, how do you feel about compliments – (1) giving them and (2) receiving them – with the following people: • just one friend of the same sex as you? • just one friend of the opposite sex? • a mixed group of friends? • new people at a casual occasion? • workplace people in a formal setting such as a meeting?				
Criticism and complaints On a scale of 1–10, where 1 is difficult and 10 is easy, how do you feel about criticism and complaints – (1) giving them and (2) receiving them – with the following people: • a member of your family? • a friend? • staff at a small café? • management staff at the place where you work? • the management of a large chain store? • the management of a large organisation such as a school or hospital?				

Strategy	Initial Score & Date	Date I observed others using this strategy / Comments	Date I used this strategy / Other comments	Final Score & Date
Reminiscing and reflecting On a scale of 1–10, where 1 is difficult and 10 is easy, how do you feel about reminiscing and reflecting with: • parents? • siblings? • grandparents and elderly people in general? • old school friends? • newer friends with a shorter history?				
Being optimistic On a scale of 1–10, where 1 is pessimistic and 10 is optimistic, how do you feel about being optimistic with the following people: • just one friend? • a group of friends? • relatives at a family gathering? • a new acquaintance? • a person in authority? • an organisation?				
Being positive about other people On a scale of 1–10, where 1 is awkward and 10 is perfectly comfortable, how do you feel about remaining positive about someone despite the disparaging remarks of:				

APPENDIX 1

Strategy	Initial Score & Date	Date I observed others using this strategy Comments	Date I used this strategy Other comments	Final Score & Date
• just one friend? • a group of friends? • a member of your family? • all of your family?				
Argument, making a point and detachment from your opinions On a scale of 1–10, where 1 is very uncomfortable and 10 is perfectly comfortable, how do you feel about coping with disagreements and arguments with: • just one friend? • a group of friends? • relatives at a family gathering? • a person in authority? • an organisation?				
Apologies and repairing conversational 'gaffes' On a scale of 1–10, where 1 is very uncomfortable and 10 is perfectly comfortable, how do you feel about apologising and repairing conversational 'gaffes', and how do you cope if someone makes a conversational blunder against you? This could be something such as calling you the wrong name. How easy is this skill with the following types of people: • family members?				

177

The Conversation Strategies Manual

Escaping!

On a scale of 1–10, where 1 is awkward and 10 is perfectly comfortable, how do you feel about politely closing a conversation and getting away from:

- just one friend who you meet on the street when you are in a hurry to catch a bus?
- a member of your family chatting at home when you want to go out to meet some friends?
- a person on their own chatting to you at a party when you want to talk to some friends you haven't seen for ages?
- an elderly neighbour who always pops out and tries to engage you in a lengthy conversation when you want to get home?
- a phone call from someone you like, but who is a 'rambler'?
- an ex-girlfriend/boyfriend who keeps phoning or chatting to you at work/university/school?
- a telephone salesperson?
- a friend or family member who keeps chatting once the film has started?
- one close friend?
- a group of friends?
- a new person in a formal situation such as an interview?

Strategy	Initial Score & Date	Date I observed others using this strategy / Comments	Date I used this strategy / Other comments	Final Score & Date

APPENDIX 1

Strategy	Initial Score & Date	Date I observed others using this strategy Comments	Date I used this strategy Other comments	Final Score & Date
Electronic conversations On a scale of 1–10, where 1 is very uncomfortable and 10 is perfectly comfortable, how do you feel about having a conversation by texting, emailing or Skyping and reporting on your activities by blog or twitter with: • members of your family? • friends? • authority figures? • strangers?				
Eavesdropping On a scale of 1–10, where 1 is dubious/uncomfortable and 10 is perfectly comfortable, how do you feel about listening in to other people's chat when you are: • alone on the bus or train and someone is speaking loudly on their mobile phone? • alone on the bus or train and some rowdy football supporters are joking with each other? • alone on the bus or train and people are talking to each other in normal or slightly quiet voices? • at a social gathering and you are in one group but you are distracted by and can easily hear the chat of another group? • (a) alone and (b) with one friend at a restaurant where the tables are rather close together and people at the next table are talking?				

Strategy	Initial Score & Date	Date I observed others using this strategy / Comments	Date I used this strategy / Other comments	Final Score & Date
• in department store or motorway restrooms where people often arrive in pairs? • outside a room in which people are having a meeting? • also, how do you feel if you find someone eavesdropping on you? **Conversation at parties and special occasions** On a scale of 1–10, where 1 is difficult and 10 is easy, how do you feel about adjusting your conversational style according to a particular occasion (depending on which apply to you), for example, at: • a party with a group of friends? • a family gathering? • a birthday party at a nightclub? • a works Christmas party? • an end-of-college/university farewell party or school prom? • a Valentine's Day party?				

APPENDIX 2: QUESTION DICE

Materials needed

- 10cm-deep upholsterery foam
- Indelible ink pen

Preparation

Cut the foam into 10cm cubes. Some upholsterers will cut the sponge for you, but if not, it's easiest to cut it with a bread knife.

Suggestion: make several as these sorts of cubes are useful for the topic-shifting dice too.

Note: Alternatively you may be able to buy blank dice or children's building blocks.

Completing the cubes

On each face of one of the dice write one of these question beginners: Who, What, Where, When, Why, How. (You could write other word classes – adverbs, conjunctions etc on the other cubes, to use in other games.)

Procedure

Take turns to roll the dice and ask another member of the group a question beginning with the word on the face of the dice. The client who is answering should give a brief response and then take their turn at asking someone else a question.

You could develop this by presenting photo-cards of people carrying out various occupations/activities and pretend that they are actually present within the group, and think up questions to ask them. Discuss their possible responses.

APPENDIX 3: SAVE YOUR CRACKER JOKES

Most cracker jokes are based on puns and idioms. Humour, even the corny pun, adds to enjoyment of life. It is possible to dismantle these simple jokes, explain them step by step, and then put them back together again, thereby making them more accessible and enjoyable.

Beware: for some reason the most groan-making jokes are the ones that seem to be most easily remembered and will be re-quoted long afterwards!

Materials needed

As many cracker jokes as you can possibly get. Within a brand of cracker they tend to repeat the same jokes, so it is a good idea to ask your friends and acquaintances to save their cracker jokes too so that you stand more chance of acquiring many different jokes. You can, of course, find books of puns as an alternative source.

Procedure

Carefully pick out the jokes you are going to work with; you are looking for the ones with obvious puns and idioms. Stick the jokes, well spaced out, on pieces of A4 and make photocopies for each group member.

The core of the work is to find the word or idiomatic phrase that means two things, the 'double entendre'. For example, look at this old joke:

Patient: *"Doctor, Doctor, I feel like a pair of curtains."*

Doctor: *"Well pull yourself together then."*

It is the words 'pull yourself together' which mean two things; in one sense we take the words literally, as in pulling curtains, and in the other sense we mean 'take control of your behaviour'. This double meaning is the key to the joke, sometimes missed so that the pun is lost. Discuss the idiomatic meaning and recap the other, literal one. Then one group member retells the joke.

What about another old one: "My dog's got no nose", "How does he smell then?", "Terrible". Here the pun is with the word 'smell'. This is an easier one to explain as no idioms are involved, just two meanings of the one word.

Once everyone is familiar with the procedure for finding the pun word another group member picks out the next pun in the same way.

BIBLIOGRAPHY AND RECOMMENDED FURTHER READING

Adams D (2009) *The Hitchhiker's Guide to the Galaxy*, Macmillan Children's Books, London.

Aston M (2003) *Aspergers in Love: Couple Relationships and Family Affairs*, Jessica Kingsley, London and Philadelphia.

Attwood T (2007) *The Complete Guide to Asperger's Syndrome*, Jessica Kingsley, London and Philadelphia.

Berger S & Hawkins G (2006) *Ready Made*, Thames & Hudson, Berkeley, CA.

Buzan T & Buzan B (2003) *The Mind Map Book*, BBC Worldwide Limited, London.

Carnegie D (2006) *How to Win Friends and Influence People*, Vermilion, London.

Gajewski N, Hirn P & Mayo P (1998) *Social Skills Strategies, a social-emotional curriculum for adolescents, Books A and B*, Thinking Publications, Eau Claire, Wisconsin.

Jack A (2004) *Red Herrings and White Elephants: The Origins of the Phrases We Use Every Day*, Metro Publishing, London.

Kelly A (1997) *Talkabout: A Social Communication Skills Package*, Speechmark, Bicester, Oxon.

Lowndes L (1999) *How to Talk to Anyone*, Thorsons, London.

Milne AA, illustrated by Shepard EH (1983) *The World of Christopher Robin*, Methuen Children's Books, London.

Pease A (1997) *Body Language, 3rd edn*, Sheldon Press, London.

Rees N (1981) *Eavesdroppings. Bizarre Overheard Remarks*, Unwin, London.

Roberts A (2011) *Here's One I Made Earlier*, Speechmark, Milton Keynes.

Roberts A & Roberts A (2009) *How Do I ... Get a Job*, Speechmark, Milton Keynes.

Roberts A & Roberts A (2009) *How Do I ... Date*, Speechmark, Milton Keynes.

Stuart-Hamilton I (2004) *An Asperger Dictionary of Everyday Expressions*, Jessica Kingsley, London and Philadelphia.